The ESSENTIALS® of
REGISTERED TRADEMARK

DATA STRUCTURES II

GW00504870

Rev. Dennis C. Smolarski, S.J., Ph.D.
Associate Professor of Mathematics
Santa Clara University, California

This book is a continuation of *"THE ESSENTIALS OF DATA STRUCTURES I"* and begins with Chapter 9. It covers the usual course outline of Data Structures II. Earlier/basic topics are covered in *"THE ESSENTIALS OF DATA STRUCTURES I"*.

Research and Education Association
61 Ethel Road West
Piscataway, New Jersey 08854

THE ESSENTIALS
OF DATA STRUCTURES II ®

Printed in the United States of America

Library of Congress Catalog Card Number 90-60324

International Standard Book Number 0-87891-837-X

WHAT "THE ESSENTIALS" WILL DO FOR YOU

This book is a review and study guide. It is comprehensive and it is concise.

It helps in preparing for exams, in doing homework, and remains a handy reference source at all times.

It condenses the vast amount of detail characteristic of the subject matter and summarizes the **essentials** of the field.

It will thus save hours of study and preparation time.

The book provides quick access to the important facts, principles and concepts in the field.

Materials needed for exams can be reviewed in summary form – eliminating the need to read and re-read many pages of textbook and class notes. The summaries will even tend to bring detail to mind that had been previously read or noted.

This "ESSENTIALS" book has been prepared by an expert in the field, and has been carefully reviewed to assure accuracy and maximum usefulness.

Dr. Max Fogiel
Program Director

CONTENTS

This book is a continuation of *"THE ESSENTIALS OF DATA STRUCTURES I"* and begins with Chapter 9. It covers the usual course outline of Data Structures II. Earlier/basic topics are covered in *"THE ESSENTIALS OF DATA STRUCTURES I"*.

CHAPTER 9

SETS

9.1   BASIC DEFINITIONS

A **set** is an ADT (abstract data type) that consists of zero or more distinct items and that lacks any inherent ordering. The standard mathematical notation for sets is a pair of curly braces that enclose an exhaustive listing of the elements contained in that set. For example, the set that consists of the two integers 3 and 5 is written {3, 5}. Since a set lacks any ordering, {3, 5} is the same set as {5, 3}. Since a set contains distinct items, there are no duplicates among the items in a set. Either an item is a member of a set or it is not — there can never be multiple copies of any item in a set. Thus, {3, 3, 5} is normally never written, since it conveys the same information as {3, 5}.

A set that contains no items is called the *empty set* or the *null set* and is frequently written φ or { }. If a set contains a subrange of some enumerable collection of items, such as letters or integers, an ellipsis can be indicated instead of an exhaustive listing. For example, {1, ... , 100} indicates the set of the first one hundred non-negative integers.

101

9.2 OPERATIONS ON SETS AND ITEMS

As with other ADTs, two elementary operations that can be performed on a set (to modify it) and on an item that can be contained in a set are the operations of *inserting* a single new item into an existing set, and of *deleting* an item from a set.

Another operation is that of determining whether an item is in a set or not. This is sometimes called the *member* or *element-of* or *in* function. Note that since a set lacks inherent ordering, there is no operation to determine where an item resides in a set.

9.3 OPERATIONS ON TWO SETS

The simple operations of inserting and deleting are usually combined into functions that operate on two sets (rather than on a set and an item of a set). The most common of these operations are *union*, *intersection*, and *difference*.

Given sets A and B, the *union* of A and B, written $A \cup B$, is the new set that contains any element that was in A along with any element that was in B. (As mentioned above, duplicates are omitted.) Thus if $A = \{3, 4, 5\}$ and $B = \{5, 6, 7\}$, then $A \cup B = \{3, 4, 5, 6, 7\}$,

The *intersection* of A and B, written $A \cap B$, is the new set that contains any element that was in A as well as in B. Thus if $A = \{3, 4, 5\}$ and $B = \{5, 6, 7\}$, then $A \cap B = \{5\}$.

The *difference* of A and B, written $A - B$, is the new set that contains any element that was in A and was not in B. Thus if $A = \{3, 4, 5\}$ and $B = \{5, 6, 7\}$, then $A - B = \{3, 4\}$.

9.4 RELATIONS BETWEEN TWO SETS

Given sets A and B, A and B are said to be *equal* if every element of A is in B and every element of B is in A. This relation is written $A = B$.

A is said to be a *subset* of B, if every element of A is an element of B. A is also said to be contained in B. This is written $A \subset B$. Note that if $A = B$, it is also true that $A \subset B$.

A is said to be a *superset* of B, if every element of B is an element of A. A is also said to contain B. This is written $A \supset B$. Note that if $A \supset B$, it is also true that $B \subset A$.

9.5 IMPLEMENTATION OF SETS

Sets usually contain a relatively small number of items, and these items are in some sense of the same category, for example, integers, letters, names, days, months, etc. In most categories there is usually some maximum number of items possible, and some way to enumerate the items (usually in some natural order). The set of all possible items in a specific category is sometimes called the *universe*. As was mentioned above, it must also be remembered that the fundamental question is whether an item is a member of a set or not.

One way of implementing sets, given these background considerations, is to use the underlying ADT of a one-dimension array (i.e., a vector) of type boolean (logical) (or of type integer). The array is declared to be of a size large enough to hold all elements of the category from which items will be stored in that set. Each cell of the array corresponds to one possible element in the general category of items. If the set contains a certain item, the cell of the array corresponding to that item is given the value of *true* (or 1); otherwise, it has a value of *false* (or 0).

This implementation is sometimes called a *bit-vector* implementation, since each element in the vector (one dimension array) is used as a signal bit to indicate the presence or absence of an element in the set.

Sets that contain elements from the same category (e.g., integers) would have the same underlying data type. However, sets that contain elements from different categories (e.g., letters and integers) would need different underlying data types.

Although sets themselves have no order, an enumerating order is usually imposed on the entire collection of elements in a specific set category (i.e., the set's universe) to simplify implementation. For example, the digits have a natural ordering. The type for a **digitset** can be defined as

ARRAY [0 .. 9] OF BOOLEAN.

If variable *a* has been declared to be of type digitset, to check whether digit 2 is in set *a*, element *a*[3] is checked. However, if a set contains another type of item, for example, the days of the week, an auxiliary function is usually used to determine the corresponding array location. This is illustrated as follows:

```
TYPE   days = (sun, mon, tues, wed, thurs, fri, sat);
       setofdays = ARRAY [1 .. 7] OF BOOLEAN;
VAR b : setofdays;

FUNCTION Daysplace (day:days) : INTEGER;
BEGIN
        CASE day OF
                sun    : Daysplace := 1;
```

104

```
            mon    : Daysplace := 2;
            tues   : Daysplace := 3;
            wed    : Daysplace := 4;
            thurs  : Daysplace := 5;
            fri    : Daysplace := 6;
            sat    : Daysplace := 7
        END
END;
```

Then, for example, to check whether set b contains tues, the value of item b[Daysplace(tues)] is checked.

Inserting an item in a set would require that the corresponding cell in the underlying array be set to true. Deleting an item in a set would require that the corresponding cell in the underlying array be set to false. Testing for the presence of an item in a set would require that the corresponding cell be checked for the value of true.

The union of two sets could be accomplished by performing the logical operation of *or* with corresponding elements of the two arrays, as the following code shows:

```
TYPE   someset = ARRAY [1. . 25] OF BOOLEAN;
VAR    a, b, c : someset;

PROCEDURE Union(a, b:someset; var c:someset);
(* c is returned as the union of sets a and b *)
VAR    i:INTEGER;
BEGIN
        FOR i := 1 TO 25 DO
            c[ i ] := a[ i ] OR b[ i ]
END;
```

Similarly, the intersection of two sets can be implemented

by performing the logical operation of *and* with corresponding elements of the two arrays.

Using the definition of subset given above, a function to test whether set a is a subset of b could be implemented as follows:

```
FUNCTION Subset(a, b : someset) : BOOLEAN;
VAR    i:INTEGER;
       check : BOOLEAN;
BEGIN
       check := TRUE;
       i := 1;
       while (i <= 25) AND check DO
            BEGIN
                IF a[ i ] THEN check := b[ i ];
                i := i + 1
            END;
            Subset : check
END;
```

Any function that checks to see whether a is a subset of b needs to check that every item in set a (i.e., every cell in a that has the value of true) is also in set b (i.e., the corresponding cell in b also has a true value). The assignment check := b[i] is executed only if a[i] is true (i.e., if item i is in set a), check becomes false only if b[i] is false, i.e., item i is not in set b.

Although this bit-vector implementation of sets may appear cumbersome, involving an auxiliary place-location function and large storage arrays, it is often preferred for many applications to various alternatives. For example, sets can also be implemented using a linked list. This implementation can save on storage since each list would only contain the amount of space needed for elements contained in the set (and pointers to other nodes). However, implementing the set operations of union, intersection and difference would be significantly more difficult.

9.6 SETS IN PASCAL

Pascal allows a programmer to define a new data type to be a set of a specific *user-defined* or *standard* type (with the exception of reals). For example,

```
TYPE
        days = (sun,mon,tues,wed,thur,fri,sat);
        setofdays = SET OF days;
        setofdigits = SET of 0 . . 9;
        setofletters = SET OF 'a' . . 'z';
```

Variables can then be declared to be of specific set types.

Constant sets are indicated by enclosing items in square brackets, with the null set being merely the brackets without any items inside. For example,

```
        months:= [  ] ;
        numbers := [1. . 4, 6];

        vowels := ['a', 'e', 'i', 'o', 'u'];
```

Union is indicated by +, intersection by ∗, and difference by −. The boolean test to determine whether an item is a member of a set is performed by using the operator *in* as follows:

```
        If 'a' IN vowels THEN ...
```

One can also use <= to test whether one set is a subset of another, or = to test for equality.

CHAPTER 10

TREES

10.1 BASIC DEFINITIONS

A **tree** can be considered to be a version of the ADT of a linked list in which each node can point to more than one other node, but no node has two or more nodes pointing to it. Thus, a tree can be viewed as a generalized list, and a singly linked list can be seen as a special case of a tree.

A **binary tree** is a tree in which each node points to at most two other nodes.

The head node of a tree is called its *root*.

The tail modes of a tree are called its *leaves*.

Nodes on trees are given relationship names based on the long-standing use of trees to keep genealogy records. Thus, the nodes pointed to by some node are called the children, sons, daughters, or offspring of that node, and the node that points to other nodes is called the parent, father, mother, or ancestor of those nodes.

Other family relationships are also used as if the tree were a family genealogy tree, i.e., the "family" relationships between nodes of a tree are labeled as grandparent, grandchild, uncle, (co-)siblings, (first) cousins, second cousins twice removed, etc. At any node, every offspring starts a new **branch** from its parent node.

The root of a tree is said to be at level *0*. Its immediate descendants are at level *1*, etc.

The **degree** of a node is the number of its offspring.

A collection of trees is termed a *forest* or an **orchard**.

A **complete** binary tree of level *n* is a tree such that at level *n*, each node is a leaf and at level *n* − 1 (or less), each node has both left and right offspring.

The **depth** (sometimes called the **height**) of a tree is the maximum level of all its leaves. The **ply** of a tree is the number of nodes in its longest branch, and equals depth + 1.

Trees are commonly depicted with the root at the top of a diagram and branches going downwards (the opposite of the way trees grow in nature). The following examples are meant to illustrate some of the definitions just presented.

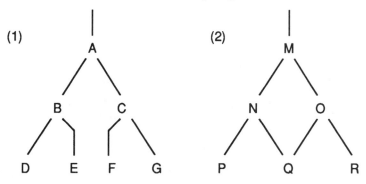

(1) and (3) are trees.
(2) is NOT a tree since Q has two nodes pointing to it.
(1) is complete, but (3) is **not** complete.

A is the root of tree (1).
B is the parent of D.
A is the grandparent of F.
E and F are (first) cousins.
X is the nephew/niece of W and W is the aunt/uncle of X.
D, E are (co-)siblings
V is of degree 2.
Y is of degree 1.
(3) is of depth 3.
V is in level 1.
The leaves of tree (1) are D, E, F, and G.

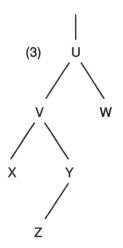

10.2 TRAVERSING BINARY TREES

There is a unique inherent order in a singly linked list, namely the order that starts at the head node and ends at the tail node. There are no real options in traversing (i.e., going to each one of) the nodes of such a list, since each node points to only one other node. Thus, it is a trivial task to list the elements of a singly linked list in linear order.

A tree is graphically represented in two dimensions by necessity. What is needed is a logical method of listing the (contents of the) nodes of a tree in one dimension (i.e., linearly). Since trees are two-dimension structures in some sense similar to two-dimension arrays, there are options in the way that information in such a structure can be listed in linear order (see Section 3.4). Thus, different linear orderings do exist for the

110

same binary (two-dimension) tree, even though only one tree is being traversed.

There are three standard orders for traversing the nodes of a tree and these correspond to the three standard ways of writing arithmetic expressions (see Appendix D). In each order, a parent and its two children (left child before the right) are listed. The names of the orders are based on whether the parent is listed before (pre–), between (in–), or after (post–) its children. On a larger tree, the same order scheme is recursively used on each node that has children.

(1) PREORDER: *parent*, left child, right child.

(2) INORDER: left child, *parent*, right child.

(3) POSTORDER: left child, right child, *parent*.

It is emphasized once again that this is not a way to obtain three different trees out of one tree. This is a way to take one (two-dimension) tree and obtain three different linear (one-dimension) listings of the nodes contained in that tree. An example of one tree and its three different traversals follows:

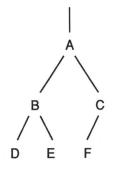

(1) PREORDER: *A* B D E C F

(2) INORDER: D B E *A* F C

(3) POSTORDER: D E B F C *A*

Notice that the root A (emphasized in the three listings) occurs in its "correct" place (before, between, after) relative to the other nodes. Also notice that if a node is missing (as with the

111

right child of C), its proper place is noted but nothing appears in the listing. (i.e., the inorder traversal of the subtree $C - F$ is $F - C$ rather than $C - F$ since the right child is missing rather than the left.)

A tree is frequently used to describe an arithmetic expression (where the leaves are variables or numbers and interior nodes are always the operators). The following is such an example.

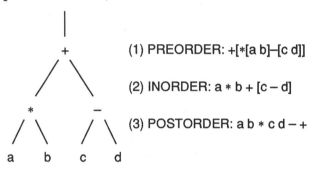

(1) PREORDER: +[*[a b]–[c d]]

(2) INORDER: a * b + [c – d]

(3) POSTORDER: a b * c d – +

The square brackets have been included for readability, and to help recognize that the three tree traversal orders correspond to the three methods of describing a mathematical binary function: prefix (functional), infix (arithmetic), and postfix (Reverse Polish Notation, "RPN") notations. However, the ultimate meaning of the expression is the same no matter what the form in which it is written.

There is one other traversal order, called *level order traversal*, which is used in special situations (see Heap sort and Section 11.1.3). In this traversal scheme, all elements of one level are listed left to right, starting with the root in level 0, and proceeding level by level until the last one. A level order traversal of the first tree in the example above would give: A B C D E F and of the second tree would give: + * – a b c d. Unlike the three other traversals, a level order traversal cannot be implemented recursively, but is usually simply implemented using a queue.

Traversal algorithms are important since they are related to searching algorithms — if information is desired in some data structure (whether an array or a tree), there needs to be some systematic way to check each node of the structure to retrieve and possibly modify the information stored there. A traversal algorithm provides a systematic procedure by which every node in an ADT can be guaranteed to be checked.

10.3 OPERATIONS ON TREES

10.3.1 POINTER IMPLEMENTATION AND EXAMPLE

The ADT of a tree is usually implemented using pointer variables although a linear implementation with arrays is also possible. The pointer variable code for trees is similar to the code for linked lists in Section 6.3.1, except that there are two "next" fields.

```
TYPE   tree   =  ^node;
       node   =  RECORD
                    left : tree
                    info : INTEGER;
                    right : tree
                 END;
```

The following sample code that uses this definition of a tree node consists of three segments: a tree generator, a tree printer (in inorder), and a driver main program. The generator segment recursively generates a tree of depth n by creating a node and then generating two trees of depth $n - 1$ which it points to. The information section of each node is filled with a number corresponding to the order of its creation, i.e., the root node contains a 1. Code such as this is primarily for demonstration purposes

113

similar to the code found in Section 6.2.7 and would rarely be used in a major program.

GENERATING A COMPLETE TREE OF DEPTH N

```
FUNCTION Gentree(n:INTEGER):tree;
(*      Recursive function to generate a complete tree of depth n.
        The nodes are labeled from 1 to 2^n-1 in the order
        created. *)
VAR t : tree;
BEGIN
        New(t);
        numnode := numnode + 1; (* note that numnode is a
                global variable *)
        t^.info := numnode;
        IF n <= 0    THEN t^.left := NIL
                     ELSE t^.left := Gentree(n-1);
        IF n <= 0    THEN t^.right := NIL
                     ELSE t^.right := Gentree(n-1);
        Gentree := t
END;    (* Gentree *)
```

PRINTING A TREE — INORDER

```
PROCEDURE Inprint(t:tree);
(*      Recursive procedure to print a tree in Inorder traversal
        — left, parent, right *)
BEGIN
        IF t <> NIL THEN
            BEGIN
                Inprint (t^.left);
                Write(t^.info);
                Inprint(t^.right)
            END
END;
```

MAIN PROGRAM

```
BEGIN
        numnode := 0;
        Inprint (Gentree(4))
END.
```

The code for Inprint can be easily modified by re-arranging the center three lines if a routine to print a preorder or postorder traversal is desired.

10.3.2 ORDERED TREES

Trees can be used for ordering purposes. First of all, the traversal order to be used and the resulting output order must be chosen. The common *traversal* used is *inorder*, and the desired resulting order of the linear listing of the nodes is commonly $l < p < r$ which results in numerical or alphabetical order.

A tree whose node contents are such that the inorder traversal results in an ordered linear listing is called a *lexicographically ordered tree* or a lexically ordered tree (or a binary search tree). A lexicon is another name for a dictionary. Thus, this is equivalent to saying the tree is in "dictionary" or "alphabetical" order. Example:

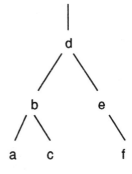

The inorder traversal of this tree gives the linear list of: a b c d e f , i.e., alphabetical order. Thus, this is a lexicographically ordered tree.

A binary tree that is lexicographically ordered can be an efficient alternative to an array for ordered data storage, especially if many insertions

115

and deletions take place with the stored data. What are needed are efficient ways to insert and retrieve (or find) information in such a tree. The following section describes an algorithm for inserting an item into an ordered tree. A retrieval algorithm can be obtained by modifying this insertion algorithm slightly. A second comparison line is added before the present one and this new comparison would test for equality (and return a pointer to the "found" node). Instead of inserting a new node when reaching a nil-pointer, a retrieval algorithm returns a "not found." This retrieval algorithm is essentially a tree version of binary search (see Section 5.2), each time eliminating half of the tree from further consideration.

10.3.3 INSERTING INTO AN ORDERED TREE

Any algorithm for inserting new items into a lexicographically ordered tree must retain the ordering in the enlarged tree. The following is one version of such an algorithm.

ALGORITHM TO INSERT AN ITEM INTO AN ORDERED TREE
—Choose root to be the initial COMPARE-NODE
—REPEAT
      (∗ Compare item-to-be-inserted
         with contents of COMPARE-NODE ∗)
     —IF item-to-be-inserted > COMPARE-NODE contents
       THEN IF right child of COMPARE-NODE exists
           THEN choose the right child
             as the new COMPARE-NODE
           ELSE insert item as new right child
             and STOP!
       ELSE IF left child of COMPARE-NODE EXISTS
           THEN choose the left child
             as the new COMPARE-NODE
           ELSE insert item as new left child
             and STOP!
— UNTIL item has been inserted.

116

10.3.4 EXAMPLE: REPEATED INSERTIONS INTO AN ORDERED TREE

The following example starts with an empty tree, and repeatedly inserts items into the tree so that at each point, the tree is always lexicographically ordered. In other words, at every point, if an inorder traversal of the tree is performed, the output list of items will be in alphabetical order.

INPUT LIST: N S I A L P J M

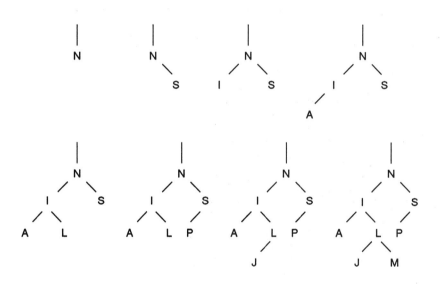

10.3.5 DELETING FROM AN ORDERED TREE

Any algorithm for deleting a node from a lexicographically ordered tree must retain the ordering in the reduced tree. However, this task is more difficult than in the case of the insertion algorithm. Given the following tree:

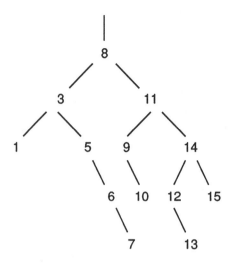

the way nodes 15, 5, or 11 are deleted differ drastically. The procedure used depends on whether the node has no children (i.e., is a leaf), has only one child, or has two children.

A) If the node-to-be-deleted has no children (i.e., is a leaf), merely delete it. (See deleting 15.)

B) If the node-to-be-deleted has only one child, the descendants of that node are each moved up one level, so that the child takes the place of the deleted node. (See deleting 5 — the right descendant of 3 is now 6.)

C) If the node-to-be-deleted has both children, a major adaptation to the tree takes place:

    1) The inorder successor to the node-to-be-deleted is identified. Note that the inorder successor cannot have a left child, else that (left) child would be the actual inorder successor. If node 11 is to be deleted in the tree above, its inorder successor is 12 (which has no left child).

2) Replace the node-to-be-deleted with its inorder successor.

3) Replace the inorder successor with its right child (if it exists) (and move all successive descendants up one level). Since the inorder successor has not left child (see 1 above), there are no left descendants to have to worry about.

After deleting 11 in the previous example, the tree looks like:

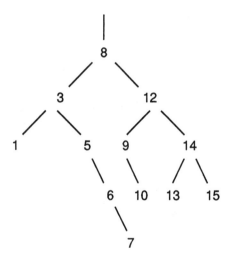

The deletion algorithm will also work if the inorder predecessor takes the place of the deleted node, with necessary changes to the rest of step (C). The final tree will be ordered, but will be a different tree than that which appears here.

10.4 BALANCING AND ROTATING

A *balanced binary tree* is one in which for every node, the heights of the two subtrees do not differ by more than 1. A balanced binary tree is also called an *AVL-tree*, named for

Georgii M. Adelson-Velskii and Yevgenii M. Landis (who developed a height-balancing algorithm in 1962).

Balancing is the process of converting an arbitrary tree into a balanced tree.

The ***balance factor*** of a node is the height of the left rooted branch minus the height of the right rooted branch. By "left (or right) rooted branch" is meant the left subtree from the node including the node. (Thus, for example, if a node has no left child, the left rooted branch consists of that node alone and has height 0.)

THEOREM

In a balanced binary tree, each node has a balance factor of either −1, 0, or 1.

PROBLEM

Insertions and deletions in a (lexicographically ordered) binary tree may make it highly imbalanced, so that searching for an item (in two different ordered trees, both containing the same set of items) may vary drastically in the number of steps. For example, the two following trees are both ordered and both

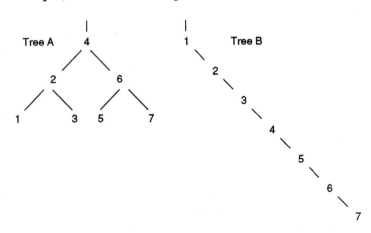

120

contain the same inforamtion, but have drastically different shapes.

Tree A and tree B both have the same inorder traversal, but tree B is, in a sense, a degenerate tree and is equivalent to a singly linked list.

To find 3, 5, or 7 in tree A would only take 3 comparisons (at maximum) using the search algorithm mentioned earlier in Section 10.3.2. However, in tree B, it takes 3 comparisons to find 3, 5 to find 5, and 7 to find 7.

For some applications, it can be important to be able to search quickly, so it is important to make a tree as balanced as possible.

Balancing is accomplished by performing an action called *rotation* about certain nodes.

A *simple rotation* about a node is a rearrangement of a subtree rooted at that node such that the inorder traversal remains the same and one of the children of the node has now become the root (of that subtree).

A *right [left] rotation* is one in which the root has become the right [left] child of the new root (which was formerly the

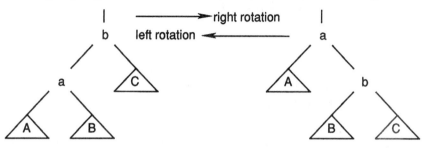

Note: Subtree B switches parents!

121

left [right] child of the old root). In the process, one of the subtrees switches parents as depicted in the diagram above.

The process of a left rotation can be coded simply as follows:

```
PROCEDURE Leftrotate (VAR a:tree);
VAR b,temp:tree;
BEGIN
        b:=a^.right;
        temp := b^.left;
        b^.left := a;
        a^.right := temp;
        a:= b
END;
```

What follows is a general description of a *balancing algorithm* for ordered trees. It does not take into account special situations.

1) After an insertion/deletion, check balance factors of the various nodes from the point of insertion/deletion to the root.

2) If the balance factor = 2 for a node, rotate right.

3) If the balance factor = − 2 for a node, rotate left.

NOTES

(a) After rotation, the balances of the nodes should be rechecked. Additional rotations may be necessary.

(b) If two nodes happen to be unbalanced in opposite directions, a double rotation in opposite directions is necessary.

122

The following is an example of a single rotation.

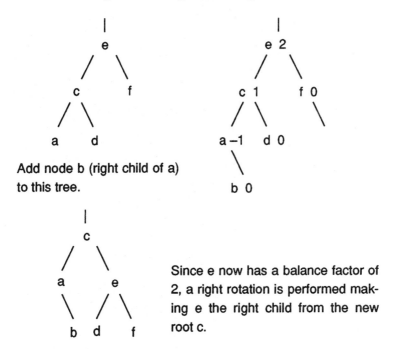

Add node b (right child of a)
to this tree.

Since e now has a balance factor of
2, a right rotation is performed making e the right child from the new
root c.

Balanced tree after rotation.

10.5 THREADING TREES

Tree traversal is a common operation and is naturally described recursively. However, if a traversal routine is not or cannot be implemented recursively, it is possible to explicitly include a stack in the routine. An explicit stack is usually more efficient. However, pushes and pops still can take more time than desired.

One common approach to increase efficiency in a traversal routine is to *thread* a tree, i.e., to insert additional links (pointers) to aid in the traversal. Commonly, these threads are added from leaves (and even other nodes that do not have both children) to the inorder successor (and/or the inorder predecessor).

Nil-pointers at nodes can be modified to indicate they are now threads or "back"-pointers. To do this, it must be determined:

1) whether a node has a nil-pointer as a pointer in either right or left child field, and

2) what the inorder successor (and predecessor) to that node is.

In addition, the definition of a tree is modified to allow more than one pointer to any node.

Tree-threading can be limited to just right (inorder) successors, if desired, obtaining a partially (inorder) threaded tree.

NOTES

(a) Threads always point to an ancestor, never to a descendant.

(b) Threads take the place of a nil-ponter (left or right child). Therefore, the total number of children and threads at any node (in a binary tree) must always equal two.

(c) A thread from the right-most node of a tree (which never has an inorder successor) points to a special header node that in turn points to the root of the tree.

(d) When depicting threads visually, in order not to be misleading, a thread is always drawn on the same side as the pointer to a child that it replaces. For example, a thread that points to the inorder successor of a node and replaces a pointer to a right child is drawn on the right side of the node.

The following are examples of a partially (inorder successor) threaded and a completely threaded tree.

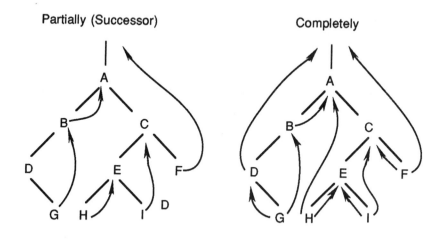

Partially (Successor)   Completely

Code for threaded trees must distinguish between threads and links to offspring. Various methods have been developed to do this. In linear implementations, the link pointer values are often negated if they are threads. Thus, by checking if a link value is negative, it can be determined whether the pointer is a thread or a link to an offspring, i.e., whether the pointer is pointing to a child or to an ancestor.

In linked implementations, (at least) one other field (which can merely be a boolean flag called *rthread*) is added to each node record, indicating whether the right link is a thread or not. Rthread is true if the right link is a thread to an ancestor, and false if it is not a thread (i.e., if it points to a child). The code for tree traversal is so written that each time a right branch is chosen, rthread is tested first to determine what action is taken next.

10.6 GENERAL TREES

The theory and use of binary trees is fairly well-developed. But things complicate rapidly if the tree is not binary. It is difficult even to decide how a tree should be stored if the maximum degree of its nodes is not known.

A standard practice to handle general trees is to transform the arbitrary tree into a binary tree (or even to transform a forest of general trees into a binary tree). The common transformation is done via what is called "Knuth(ian) natural correspondence" (named after Donald Knuth at Stanford University). The procedure is straightforward and is described as follows:

1) All co-siblings are linked together (and, given a forest, the roots of each of the trees are linked together);

2) the left-most offspring remains linked to its parent, but

3) all other links to parents are removed;

4) the transformed structure is rotated 45° clockwise to exhibit a new binary tree.

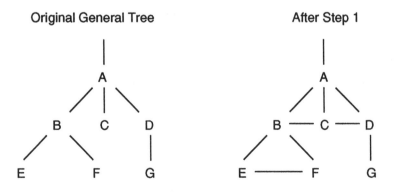

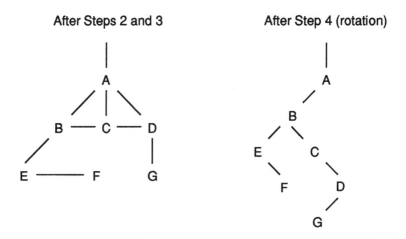

The previous is a simple example of such a transformation.

In the new tree created, some of the relationships of the original general tree can be determined. For example, a left child in the new tree corresponds to the first child in the original tree (cf. left child of A is B). A node and its right descendants in the new tree correspond to co-siblings in the original tree (see E and its left child F).

CHAPTER 11

ADVANCED SORTING

11.1 HEAP SORT

11.1.1 BASIC DEFINITIONS

Heap sort is the first sorting algorithm to be examined that does not make use of an array as its fundamental data type for its derivation and analysis. It is based on the ADT of a binary tree. Before examining the algorithm itself, some new terminology is presented.

A *strictly binary tree* is a binary tree in which every node has degree 0 or 2.

An *almost complete binary tree* is a strictly binary tree of depth $k + 1$ such that:

1) every leaf is either at level k or level $k + 1$;

2) at level k, all leaves are to the right of nodes with children, (i.e., the internal nodes).

A *heap structure* is either an almost complete binary tree of depth $k + 1$ or a modified almost complete binary tree of depth $k + 1$ such that the rightmost internal node at level k has just a left child (and, thus the tree is not strictly binary).

A *heap* is a heap structure such that the key at any node is greater than the keys at each of its (possible) descendants.

The following examples illustrate these definitions.

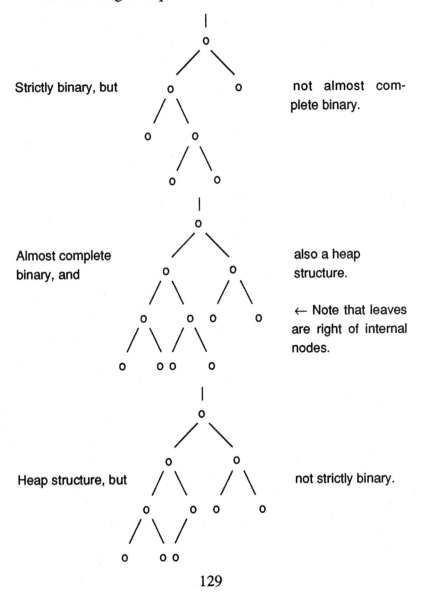

Strictly binary, but ... not almost complete binary.

Almost complete binary, and ... also a heap structure.

← Note that leaves are right of internal nodes.

Heap structure, but ... not strictly binary.

Heap.

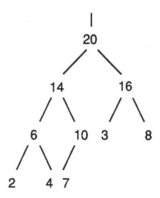

NOTES

A) In a heap, the root contains the largest key.

B) Any path from the root to a leaf is ordered. For example, in the last tree above, $20 \geq 14 \geq 10 \geq 7$.

The *Heap Sort Algorithm* consists of three major steps, the first of which is done once, and the other two repeated until the sorting is completed.

1) CREATE a heap.

2) EXCHANGE the last item of the sublist (last active leaf) with the first (root).

3) ADJUST the heap.

11.1.2 CREATING THE HEAP

There are various ways to perform this step. One way is to take elements from an input source, and add them, one by one, as new leaves to a heap structure (all the while keeping the figure a heap structure). After each insertion, the tree is adjusted to make sure it is properly ordered. Because of the nature of the structure and the fact that it was a heap before each insertion, only the path from the new leaf to the root needs to be checked and, if necessary, elements in that path re-adjusted. This algorithm is illustrated by the following example.

Input list to be sorted: 2 7 5 4 1 9 8 3
(The starred nodes indicate the only path that needs to be checked and re-adjusted if necessary.)

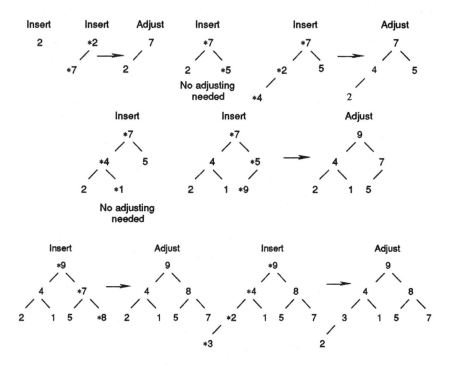

A common alternate algorithm is to put all elements into a heap structure first and then turn the structure into a heap. This process is done by looking at each parent node, starting with the rightmost parent in the next to last level, and moving right to left in each level and upwards level by level until the root is reached. Each parent is compared with its children and is ex-

131

changed with the larger of its children, if necessary. If a child itself has descendants, this process is repeated until a leaf is reached. Only one path from a parent node to a leaf offspring needs to be checked.

11.1.3 EXCHANGING ELEMENTS AND ADJUSTING

By definition, in a heap the root contains the largest item. This item can be stored by being moved to the last leaf (which is then ignored), and replacing the root with the previous contents of the last leaf. Then the heap structure needs to be adjusted back to be a heap. However, (once again) this means only having to examine one path from the root to a leaf. Starting with the root, the item in a node is exchanged with the larger of the two children, and this process is repeated either until both children are smaller than the parent node, or until a leaf has been reached.

The complete algorithm consists of a loop that repeats the exchange of the root with the "last" leaf of the "active" section of the tree and the re-adjustment of the heap structure into a heap. Each time through this exchange-adjustment step, the "active" section of the tree is shortened by one leaf. At the end, if the entire tree is traversed, in what is sometimes called a "level" order traversal (i.e., one level at a time, from left to right, starting at level 0, i.e., the root) (see Section 10.2), the elements will be in order. This algorithm is illustrated by the following example that starts with the completed tree at the end of the previous example.

(The starred nodes indicate the only path that needs to be checked and re-adjusted if necessary).

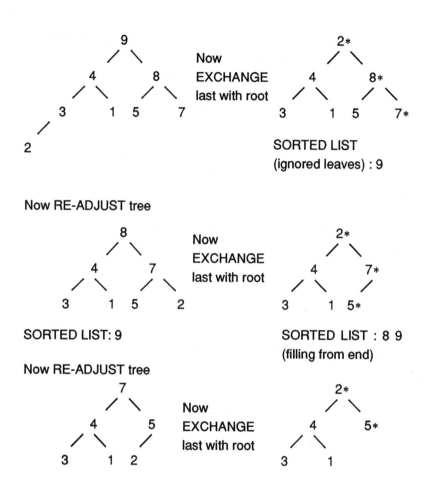

Now EXCHANGE last with root

SORTED LIST
(ignored leaves) : 9

Now RE-ADJUST tree

Now EXCHANGE last with root

SORTED LIST: 9

SORTED LIST : 8 9
(filling from end)

Now RE-ADJUST tree

Now EXCHANGE last with root

SORTED LIST: 9

SORTED LIST : 7 8 9

The rest of the steps are similar and are omitted.

11.1.4 IMPLEMENTATION

A tree that is a heap structure can be stored linearly in an array fairly simply, level by level, starting with the root at level 0. Not every tree can be stored so easily, but in a tree that is a heap structure, each level (except possibly the last) has all possible nodes, and in the last level any missing nodes are to the right of all the rest. The following heap structure has the nodes labeled according to the array locations in which they would be stored.

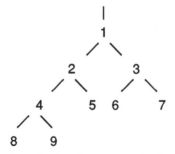

Given this tree, the relation between the locations of a node and its children can be established by doubling the parent's location (and adding 1) to get the child's location. For example,

the children of node 1 are nodes 2 and 3
the children of node 3 are nodes 6 and 7
the children of node 4 are nodes 8 and 9

Using this scheme for determining the locations of child nodes and parent nodes, heap sort is usually implemented linearly, using an array, even though the theory of trees was needed to design the algorithm.

11.1.5 BRIEF ANALYSIS

The theory of trees is also helpful in analyzing heapsort. A heap-structure is a binary tree, and a binary tree of depth m has $2^{m+1} - 1$ nodes maximum. For example,

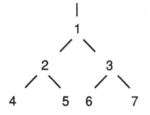

has depth 2 — THEREFORE the maximum number of nodes is $2^{2+1} - 1 = 8 - 1 = 7$

134

After the heap is set up, only elements in one path from a root to a leaf need to be examined, and this is done only once for each node. Since the length of a path, at most, is m for a tree of $2^{m+1} - 1$ nodes, this can be written as $\log_2 n$ for a tree of n nodes. The length of a path equals the (maximum) number of comparisons needed to put nodes in that path in order. Since this process of ordering is repeated for each node, the worst case amount of work needed for the heap sort algorithm is (less than) n times $\log_2 n$ or $0(n \log n)$.

Because this is significantly faster than the elementary algorithms presented in Chapter 4, heap sort is usually termed an advanced method.

To compare heap sort with an elementary method, a list of 32 items requires around 160 comparisons for heap sort, but 1024 comparisons for bubble sort (since bubble sort is an $0(n^2)$ algorithm).

11.2 QUICK SORT

Many versions of quick sort exist. Some of them are recursive while others are non-recursive in the hopes of obtaining greater efficiency. The recursive versions generally follow this pattern.

Given a list of elements in an array L as follows:

quick sort subdivides the list appropriately, and calls itself on both sections of the divided list. The subdivision of the list is done by routine *Split* which does most of the work in this algorithm. Split can be said to "semi-sort" the items in the array by re-arranging them and choosing the division point so that all the elements in the left section are less than all the elements in the right section. The following sample code shows how straightforward the overall quick sort algorithm is. For simplicity, the array to be sorted, L, is assumed to be a global variable. The two arguments, l and r, are the pointers to the left and right items in the subsection being processed.

```
PROCEDURE Quicksort(l,r:INTEGER)
VAR i:INTEGER;
BEGIN
        IF l < r THEN
            BEGIN
                Split(l,r,i);
                Quicksort(l,i–1);
                Quicksort(i+1,r)
            END
END;
```

The routine Split (sometimes called Partition or Rearrange) "semi-sorts" the elements in the array by the following steps:

1) It chooses some comparand element x.

2) It divides the list into two sections (not necessarily of equal lengths), such that,

   a) in the left (first) section, $L[1]$ to $L[i]$, each element is less than x and

   b) in the right (other) section, $L[i + 1]$ to $L[r]$, each element is greater than (or equal to) x.

There are numerous ways to code the routine Split, as well

as numerous ways to choose the comparand element x. Some of the major choices for x are: the first element in the array, the middle element, or the first element not equal to a previous element. The following diagrams and codes demonstrate one version of Split.

Array L (to be sorted):

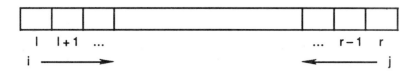

Let x be some element (see choices given above).

```
i:=l; j:=r; (* local pointers to left and right ends *)
REPEAT
        WHILE L[ j ] >= x DO j:=j−1; (* locate an item too small *)
        WHILE L[ i ] < x DO i:=i+1; (* locate an item too large *)
        IF i<=j THEN
            BEGIN (* switch misplaced items *)
                temp:=L[ j ];
                L[ j ]:=L[ i ];
                L[ i ]:=temp
            END
UNTIL j <= i;
```

Example:
First time through REPEAT loop.

```
x=5        3     2     8     5     9     4     1  (j does
(middle                                             not
element)   i ───────▶ i ──────────────────── j   move)
                        ^                       ^
```

Second time through REPEAT loop.

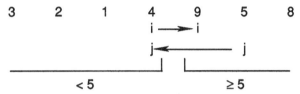

Third time through REPEAT loop (pointers cross — no exchange).

Quick sort is $O(n^2)$ for the worst case, but in the average case it is $O(n \log n)$. Tests published in the book "Data Structures + Algorithms = Programs" by Niklaus Wirth (the designer of the language Pascal) indicate that quick sort even beats heap sort by a factor of 2 to 3.

11.3 INDEX SORTING

Sometimes an auxiliary array is used in a sorting routine such that this auxiliary array modifies the indices of the actual array containing the information, and such that the items in the auxiliary array are exchanged, rather than (the possibly huge number of) items in the main array. Such a strategy is called **index sorting** (or key sorting, auxiliary array sorting, or sorting by address).

Instead of being a separate sorting scheme, this approach is used in conjunction with other standard methods. A favorite sorting scheme is actually used, but the code is modified so that items in the auxiliary array are exchanged rather than those in the main array. This strategy is especially appropriate when dealing with large records, especially when the records are stored in separate arrays (as is sometimes necessary in FOR-

TRAN or BASIC).

COMMENT

Whether one writes in FORTRAN or Pascal, the amount of work done to exchange large records is the same. However, the coding may be (deceptively) simpler in Pascal. For example, given

```
TYPE  line = RECORD
         id : INTEGER
         name : ARRAY [1 . . 30] OF CHAR;
         address : ARRAY [1 . . 30] OF CHAR;
         state: ARRAY [1 . . 2] OF CHAR;
         zip ; INTEGER
         END;

VAR list : ARRAY [1 . . 100] OF line;
     temp : line;
```

then

```
         line[ i ] := temp;
```

is actually equivalent to *64* separate assignment statements. Whether it is written out at 64 statements (FORTRAN or BASIC) or written out as one (Pascal, Modula-2, Ada), the amount of work done and the time involved is the same.

When index sorting is used, an auxiliary array is set up that contains the indices (i.e., subscripts) of the elements of the array containing the items to be sorted. Then the code of the sorting routine is modified so that (1) the elements in the information array are always accessed by means of an index array element and (2) only elements in the index array are exchanged. This process is illustrated in the following:

139

STRATEGY

(1)   compare x[index[i] with x[index[j]]
(2)   exchange index[i] with index[j] if necessary.

(**Note:** The original array x remains unchanged!)

Using the bubble sort scheme:

subscript	1	2	3	4	5
x array	15	0	1	20	4
index array	1	2	3	4	5

$\wedge$————$\wedge$————$\wedge$ $\wedge$————$\wedge$

The following comparisons are done:

x[index[1]] = x[1] = 15 ?<? x[index[2]] = x[2] = 0 NO!
Exchange index[1] and index[2]
x[index[2]] = x[1] = 15 ?<? x[index[3]] = x[3] = 1 NO!
Exchange index[2] and index[3]
x[index[3]] = x[1] = 15 ?<? x[index[4]] = x[4] = 20 ok
x[index[4]] = x[4] = 20 ?<? x[index[5]] = x[5] = 4 NO!
Exchange index[4] and index[5]

After one pass, the original array stays the same, but the index array
has been modified.

subscript	1	2	3	4	5
x array	15	0	1	20	4
index array	2	3	1	5	4

The following comparisons are done in the next pass:

140

x[index[1]] = x[2] = 0 ?<? x[index[2]] = x[3] = 1 ok
x[index[2]] = x[3] = 1 ?<? x[index[3]] = x[1] = 15 ok
x[index[3]] = x[1] = 15 ?<? x[index[4]] = x[5] = 4 NO!
Exchange index[3] and index[4]
x[index[4]] = x[1] = 15 ?<? x[index[5]] = x[4] = 20 ok

The index array now is:

subscript	1	2	3	4	5
x array	15	0	1	20	4
index array	2	3	5	1	4

The elements in the x array have now been ordered (even though only two passes were done). Notice that the index array gives this order, i.e., the second element (in the x array) is the smallest, then comes the third then the fifth then the first, and finally, the fourth (which is the largest element).

Any regular version of a sorting algorithm can be modified to be an index version. An index array must be included in the code, and the array must be initialized properly (normally such that index[i] = i). In addition, any comparison lines need to be altered so that the items are compared through the index array (as in the example above), and the switching section modified so that the elements of the index array are switched rather than the items in the main array.

CHAPTER 12

ELEMENTARY GRAPH THEORY

12.1 FUNDAMENTALS

A **graph** (or network), *G(V,E)* is an ADT that is a collection of two types of objects: *V* a set of vertices (also called nodes or points) and edges (also called arcs or lines) connecting some of the vertices together.

If an edge in *E* connects vertices v_i and v_j (both elements of *V*) together, the edge is said to be *incident* on vertices v_i and v_j. The vertices v_i and v_j are called *endpoints* of the edge. There are different ways of indicating the edge that joins vertices v_i and v_j together, most of which are self-explanatory. An edge that joins a vertex with itself is often called a *self-loop*.

If edges in a graph are given a direction, the graph is said to be a *directed graph* or *digraph*. Otherwise, the graph is said to be *undirected.* Two edges joining the same two vertices (in the same direction) are said to be *parallel.* Two vertices connected by an edge are said to be *adjacent* (or neighbors).

It is sometimes convenient to assign a weight (i.e., a number) or some other label to each of the edges in a (directed or undirected) graph. The resulting graph is called a *weighted graph* (or labeled graph or weighted network).

The following are some examples to illustrate these initial definitions.

1

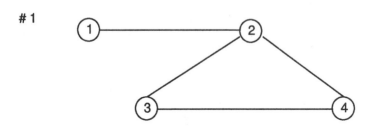

An UNdirected graph — 2,3 are adjacent, and 1, 3 are NOT adjacent.
| V | = 4.
| E | = 4.

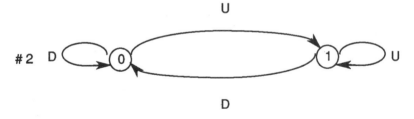

Directed Graph that is also a "labeled" graph.

This second example represents a mathematical machine (called a *finite state automaton*), and is the standard way such machines are depicted. Vertices correspond to "states" in a machine, and edges correspond to "transitions" between states. (The theory of these machines provides the basis for the study of programming languages and compiler design.) In particular, this example shows a machine that models a light switch, where 0 indicates "off," 1 indicates "on," U indicates "(turn the switch) up," and D indicates "down."

COMMENT

Graphs are used in many ways to model "real world" situations. A common use of a graph is in a road map, where the vertices are cities, and the edges are (major) roads. Graphs are also useful in determining transportation routes (e.g., airline routes), utility lines (e.g., power, water, oil, phone), and questions of rates for services. Sometimes graphs are used after a problem has been transformed. For example, adjacency of countries (states) can be checked by converting countries (states) to vertices, and common boundaries to edges between these vertices. The Konigsberg bridge problem of graph theory (see Section 12.3 below) is an example of a problem that is transformed before a solution is found.

A *path* from vertex u to vertex v is a sequence of edges, $(0, 1)$, $(1, 2)$, $(2, 3)$, ... $(n - 1, n)$, such that two successive edges are incident on a common vertex, the first edge is incident on u, and the last edge is incident on v. (There also exist directed paths in digraphs.) A path with no duplicate vertices is said to be simple. (*Note*: Some authors do not allow self-loops in paths.)

The *degree* of a vertex, abbreviated deg(v) or $d(v)$, is the number of edges incident on it. In digraphs, a distinction is made between in-degrees and out-degrees (the number of edges going into [or out of] a vertex).

If there is a path between any two vertices of a graph, that graph is said to be *connected*.

If deg(v) = 0, then v is an *isolated vertex*. Thus, if there exists a v in V, such that v is isolated, G is not connected.

If there exists a unique (simple) path between any two vertices, the graph is called a (graph-theoretic) tree.

A tree is called *rooted* (or has a root) if one vertex is designated as the root. The ADT called a "tree" in Chapter 10 is equivalent to the (graph-theoretic) "rooted tree."

A *complete graph* has an edge between every two vertices.

A *cycle* (or circuit) is a path where the first vertex and the last vertex are the same. If a graph has no cycles, it is called *acyclic*.

The *length* of a path is the number of edges in the path. In a weighted graph, the length is sometimes the sum of the weights of the edges.

A *spanning tree* is a subgraph of a connected graph, such that the edges form a tree and all vertices are incident on some edge.

A graph is *planar* if it can be so drawn in the plane that no edge crosses over another edge.

The following exmaples are meant to illustrate more of the definitions.

3

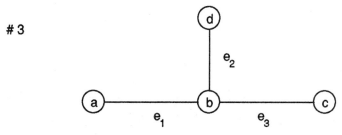

Degree(b) = 3, and degree (d) = 1.
One path from a to c is $e_1 e_3$.
a and c are not adjacent.
This graph is connected, but **not** complete.
e_1 is incident on a and b.

4

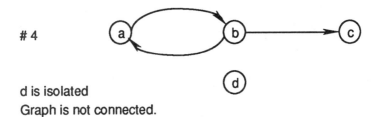

d is isolated

Graph is not connected.

5

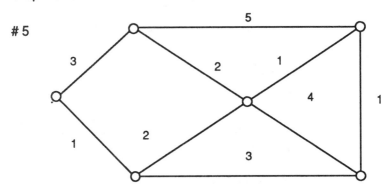

A weighted graph used, e.g., for scheduling flight prices, indicating mileage.

6

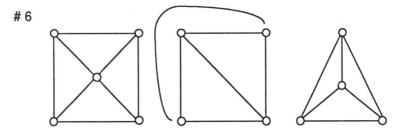

Note equivalence or non-equivalence of graphs.

These are three equivalent versions of a complete graph on 4 vertices. The right versions are planar but the leftmost is not.

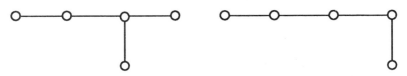

Two graphs with 5 vertices that are not equivalent.

12.2 GRAPH PROBLEMS AND ALGORITHMS

12.2.1 GRAPH TRAVERSALS

As with tree traversals (Section 10.2), since graphs are two-dimension structures, there is more than one way to list the vertices of a graph linearly. The problem becomes even more complicated with graphs than with trees because there may be more than one way of entering a vertex in a graph.

As was mentioned in other sections, traversal algorithms are related to searching algorithms. If information is desired in some data structure (whether an array or tree or graph), there needs to be some systematic way to check each vertex of the structure to retrieve and possibly modify the information stored there.

There are two standard approaches to traversing graphs: depth-first search and breadth-first search.

In a *depth-first search* algorithm, one starts out at a designated vertex and goes to any other vertex. Each time a vertex is reached and "visited," it is "marked" somehow. From the second vertex, one visits another unmarked vertex. Eventually, it may no longer be possible to go to any other unmarked vertices. At that point, one backtracks to the previous vertex and checks its other neighbors and continues the algorithm. Eventually, if the graph is connected, all vertices will be visited.

Depth-first search is implemented using a *stack* that stores the vertices visited. Past vertices are popped off the stack when they can no longer lead to other unmarked vertices. The stack thus enables backtracking to take place. The preorder traversal of a binary tree is essentially a depth-first search algorithm.

147

In a *breadth-first search* algorithm, one starts out at a designated vertex (as before), and visits all its neighbors. From these neighbors, one visits all neighbors not already marked. This process continues until all vertices are marked.

Breadth-first search is implemented using a *queue* that stores the vertices visited. Past vertices are dequeued when all of its unmarked neighbors have been enqueued. The queue thus enables the algorithm to keep track of all the neighbors visited. The level order traversal of a binary tree is essentially a breadth-first search algorithm.

12.2.2 OTHER COMMON GRAPH THEORY PROBLEMS

This section mentions some of the major problems associated with graph theory.

1. **Finding a Minimum Spanning Tree**: This algorithm discovers which edges are necessary to form a tree containing every vertex of the graph. If the graph is un-weighted, depth-first search is used. If the graph is weighted, the algorithm uses a version of breadth-first search to minimize any weights associated with the edges, by choosing the least weighted edge associated with each neighbor of a vertex.

2. **Finding a Shortest Path Between Two Points**: Usually breadth-first search can be used, with one point being the start vertex and the algorithm stopping when the second point is reached. There are versions of the algorithm both in the weighted and unweighted cases. A common application would be to find the minimal price for travel between two cities.

3. **Searching for a Vertex with a Specified Label**: Either search algorithm can be used.

4. **Finding Connected Components:** Either search algorithm can be used starting with any vertex. When the algorithm is done, the marked vertices form one component of the graph, and are removed from further consideration. Another vertex is chosen and a search algorithm is applied again.

5. **Finding "Weak" Links:** A weak link is an edge whose removal results in a disconnected graph. An application would be in discovering where in a communication network a line exists whose failure would separate one part of the network from another.

6. **Determining Planarity:** A schematic diagram of an electronic circuit on a flat surface can be considered to be a graph. Designing a circuit to avoid "wire" crossovers is equivalent to trying to find a planar version of the graph. Not every graph can be drawn planar.

7. **Coloring Graphs:** The Four Color Theorem states that in a map (e.g., the United States) only four different colors are needed to distinguish adjacent states. This can be transformed into a graph problem in which states are reduced to vertices and adjacent boundaries to edges between vertices. The coloring problem reduces to a problem of labeling the vertices so that two adjacent vertices never have the same label.

8. **Finding Maximum Flow:** Suppose a graph is a model of a water system or power system between plants and cities, and the weighted edges represent capacities of the pipes or wires. An algorithm for maximum flow tries to determine the maximum capacity possible that can "flow" from one designated *source* vertex to a designated *sink* vertex.

Two other problems, those of finding an Euler path or a Hamilton path through a graph, will be discussed in the next section.

Graph algorithms tend to be more difficult to study. There are more difficulties just in finding some algorithms that work, and fewer choices in deciding which is better. However, a few of the more common procedures do have a couple of alternatives.

12.3 EULER AND HAMILTON PATHS

A *Euler path* is a path that goes through every edge once and only once. (Such a path may actually visit some vertices more than once.)

A *Hamilton path* is a path that goes through every vertex once and only once. (Such a path may actually leave some edges untravelled.)

Two common graph problems concern the existence of such paths.

1. **Finding a Euler Path through a Graph:** This is sometimes called the Konigsberg bridge problem (explained below).

2. **Finding a Hamilton Path through a Graph:** This is sometimes called the "Traveling Salesman Problem" — trying to schedule a route in which a salesman visits every city on a schedule once and only once.

The Euler path problem is solved by using the following theorem:

A graph G contains a Euler path if every vertex is of even degree or if there are only two vertices of odd degree.

This theorem provides the solution to the well-known Konigsberg bridge problem. In Konigsberg, East Prussia (now Kaliningrad in west Russia), the river that went through the city had seven bridges connecting both sides of the river with two islands in the middle. People tried to take walks in such a way that they crossed every bridge only once but were unable to find such a path. Leonhard Euler (1707 — 1783) proved it impossible by reducing the problem to a graph theoretic problem.

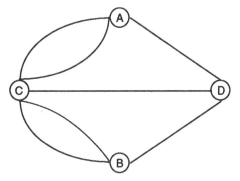

A and B are the two sections of the city on either side of the river. C and D are the two islands in the middle of the river. The edges represent the bridges between the different land masses. Note that each vertex has odd degree, contrary to Euler's theorm, so no Euler path exists.

12.4 IMPLEMENTING GRAPHS

Implementing a graph in a programming language is even more difficult than implementing a tree, since each vertex may be adjacent to an undetermined number of other vertices. Typically one of two underlying data structures are used: an **array** or a *list*. In each case, the graph is stored by keeping track of which vertices are adjacent to which other vertices. Hence, a graph data structure is usually called an *adjacency matrix* or an *adjacency (incidence) list*.

12.4.1 THE ADJACENCY MATRIX

For a graph $G(V,E)$, an n by n matrix $A = (a_{ij})$ is used, where $n = |V|$ (i.e., the number of vertices in the graph).

$$a_{ij} = \begin{cases} T \text{ (or 1) if there is an edge from } v_i \text{ to} \\ \qquad v_j \text{ in } E \\ \\ F \text{ (or 0) otherwise} \end{cases}$$

(for $1 \le i, j \le n$)

NOTES

If G is undirected, A is symmetric (therefore only about half of the matrix A needs to be stored). If G is directed, A is usually non-symmetric.

If G is weighted, then the values of the elements in A are assigned differently:

$$a_{ij} = \begin{cases} w_{ij} \quad \text{if there is an edge from } v_i \text{ to} \\ \qquad v_j \text{ in } E \text{ and } w_{ij} \text{ is the weight.} \\ \\ c \quad \text{otherwise} \end{cases}$$

where c depends on how the weights are used.

For example, if the weights represent costs, assigning c to be infinity makes sense (indicating it is very costly to try to traverse a nonexistent edge). But if the weights are capacities, c

= 0 makes sense (since if there is no edge, the capacity is zero).

The following example shows a graph and its adjacency matrix.

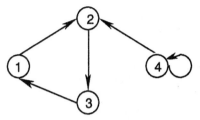

Adjacency Matrix:

	1	2	3	4
1		1		
2			1	
3	1			
4		1		1

The problem may arise in using this data structure that the resulting matrix may be very large (containing n^2 elements where n is the number of vertices) and "sparse" (i.e., has a high proportion of zeroes), and therefore wastes space in computer memory. For this reason, the adjacency list is preferred in some applications.

12.4.2 THE ADJACENCY (INCIDENCE) LIST

An adjacency list is a linked list structure with nodes of records of the form

vertex	link	or	vertex	weight	link

Each vertex has its own adjacency list associated with it, and all the vertices of a graph are usually stored together in an array (or list). The array elements form the head nodes of the

153

lists. The graph in the previous example can be represented by the following adjacency list.

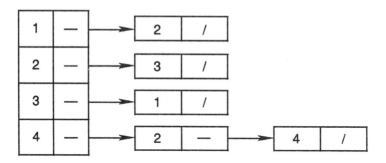

In some versions of adjacency lists, each node points back to the head node of the specific vertex in the master array. This enables a faster traversal of paths in some algorithms.

When using an adjacency list and checking whether an edge exists between two vertices, e.g., 2 and 4, an algorithm must search through a linked list associated with 2 to see if vertex 4 is in the list. In this sitaution, the list is a less efficient structure to use than a matrix where it could be checked immediately whether $a(2, 4)$ equals 1 or not without any searching.

CHAPTER 13

HASHING

13.1 RESOLVING CLASHES

Ideally, $h(x)$ is chosen to be as unique as possible, but collisions and clashes do occur, i.e., two different keys are hashed to the same number. The situation in which numerous keys are hashed to the same numbers is sometimes called *clustering*, and a good hash function avoids clustering. Yet, since it rarely can be eliminated completely, strategies are needed to resolve ambiguities that occur.

There exist several categories of techniques that attempt to resolve ambiguities. The techniques that will be examined are: *linear probing, quadratic probing, rehashing, bucket,* and *chaining*. Each technique has its own advantages and disadvantages. It should be remembered that all of them are "patch-up" techniques that try to correct problems due to collisions resulting from the hash function being used. The better the hash function, the less need there is for a highly efficient collision resolution technique.

In most collision resolution techniques, when retrieving information a search (and subsequent comparison) needs to be performed until the desired key is found. The hope is that even combining such a search with the initial hash number calculation, the total time and energy is less than occurs using a binary or linear search. Moreover, with a proper choice of a hash function, collisions can be kept to a minimum.

13.1.1 LINEAR PROBING

Linear Probing is also called *open addressing* and even, by some authors, *rehashing* (a title also used for the approach found in Section 13.1.3). The basic technique is this: suppose the information associated with key is being inserted into the storage array, but location h(key) is already in use. The algorithm then searches for the next available space and stores the information there. In other words, since h(key) is occupied, the information is stored in h(key) + 1 if that is free, or if not, then h(key) + 2, or else h(key) + 3, etc. (This procedure of looking for the next available space is called linear probing or even a rehash rule. Here "linear" is used in the same way as it is used in "linear" search, i.e., the next one in a line.)

This procedure can be described more succinctly as follows: if the location h(key) is occupied in the storage array, the first alternative space tried is h(key) + 1. However, if that is occupied also, the second alternative space tried is h(key) + 2. In general, the kth alternative space tried is h(key) + k (with wraparound of the array taken into account as usual using the mod operator).

To locate an item already stored in the array, the hash number is first computed, and the contents of that location are checked. If the item in question is not found there, then a (short) linear search is performed (starting at the computed address) until the item is found.

As an example, let h(key) equal key mod 100 + 1,

156

then $h(321) = 321 \bmod 100 + 1 = 21 + 1 = 22$
and $h(121) = 121 \bmod 100 + 1 = 21 + 1 = 22$.

The record with key 321 would be stored in location 22 in the storage array, and then linear probing done on the address for key 121, which would be stored in location 23 (if that is available).

Although straightforward, this procedure also tends to result in clustering.

13.1.2 QUADRATIC PROBING

The technique known as *quadratic probing* is similar to linear probing while trying to avoid the clustering problem. If the location $h(\text{key})$ is occupied, the first alternative space tried is the same as with linear probing, i.e., $h(\text{key}) + 1$. However, if that is occupied also, the second alternative space tried is $h(\text{key}) + 2^2$. In general, the kth alternative space tried is $h(\text{key}) + k^2$ (with wraparound of the array taken into account as usual). The gaps forced by the squared term spread out items that have the same hash number. However, it makes retrieving information already stored slightly more difficult because of the computation of the squared term.

13.1.3 REHASHING

Both linear and quadratic probing can be seen as specific examples of a more general approach usually called *rehashing* or *double hashing*. (Although sometimes "rehashing" is the name given to an algorithm that constructs a new hash table after the first one has become inefficient due to numerous deletions of elements.) This technique has several variants.

One version is a probing version, in that if $h(\text{key})$ is occupied, the kth alternative space tried is $h(\text{key}) + z_k$ (with wraparound of the array taken into account as usual). Here z_k is not simply k (as in the linear probing case) or k^2 (as in the quadratic probing case), but a more general function, such as $k * p$ where p is relatively prime to the size of the array (which ideally is a prime number as well).

Another version uses a sequence of hashing functions, h_1, h_2, h_3, etc. In other words, if $h_1(\text{key})$ is occupied, the $h_2(\text{key})$ is tried and so on, using a new hash function on the original key rather than merely modifying the first hash number obtained.

13.1.4 BUCKET

A different approach to the collision problem is taken by the **bucket** approach in which collisions are expected and integrated into the procedure. The storage array is subdivided into a number of contiguous regions called "buckets," and all records that hash to the same value are stored in the same bucket. Ideally, even though a secondary linear search is often necessary, since records with the same hash value are stored in a contiguous region, this approach can be faster than the previous three methods.

This method can be particularly useful when the number of items stored is large and an external disk file is used. The hash number can actually correspond to an address on the disk. Since disk reads are frequently done by blocks of information rather than by a single byte, the entire bucket can be read quickly from disk into fast memory for a secondary search.

13.1.5 CHAINING

Chaining is conceptually similar to the **bucket method**, and some writers refer to both methods by one title. Chaining is also called a **linked** method. It is sometimes subdivided into **separate chaining** (if a dynamic allocation of nodes in the chain is used) and *coalesced chaining* (if all the storage space has been previously declared in a linear storage scheme as in the linear implementation of lists in Section 6.2).

The basic technique is this: suppose information is being inserted into an array and location h(key) is occupied. A linked list (i.e., a "chain") is created rooted at h(key), and all records having the same hash value are stored in it. In many implementations, nothing is actually stored in the head node, since it is merely a pointer to the storage nodes that form the chain. In the following example, the hash function is h(key) = key mod 10.

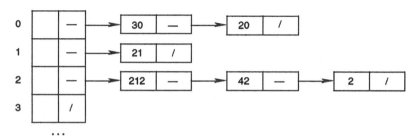

Chaining has many of the same advantages and disadvantages as does the bucket method. Both require a sequential search after the proper chain or buekct has been found. However, both avoid possibly lengthy searches (or involved calculations) that may occur with the probing methods.

CHAPTER 14

MEMORY MANAGEMENT AND GARBAGE COLLECTION

14.1 OVERVIEW

Languages that dynamically allocate space for variables (e.g., Pascal, C, LISP, Algol-68, etc.) can simplify the implementation of linked data structures such as lists, trees and graphs. Such dynamic structures with pointer variables can avoid possible overflow that may occur if a linear implementation is used. However, when working with a small machine, a long program, and a large amount of data, it is possible to run out of room for active variables, especially if dealing with linked structures with a large number of nodes. This usually results in a premature run-time termination of the program.

Often, running out of room is due to the space for nodes not being de-allocated when no longer in active use, and not merely the presence of numerous nodes. Old nodes may not be in active use, yet the space they occupy is not available for re-use.

In Pascal, nodes can be de-allocated using the procedure *dispose*. However, there is some controversy about whether dispose is a good idea. Take, for example, the following segment of code:

```
New(p);
  ...
q := p;
Dispose(p);
  ...
```

After this code segment, q points to a node that has been freed. This situation is often called a ***dangling reference*** and can be very dangerous in a program.

Because of this problem, some languages (e.g., LISP, SNOBOL) do not allow the programmer to dispose of nodes, but dispose of unused nodes internally, invisible to the programmer. Unfortunately, this automatic memory management is a time-consuming process, and thus, less efficient than the correct use of dispose. The internal memory management routine used by some languages to reclaim unused, but not de-allocated, space is usually called ***garbage collection***. Some LISP implementations explicitly tell how many times a garbage collection routine was invoked and even when the routine was invoked and completed. The purpose of such a garbage collection routine is to obtain more room for dynamic allocation of memory. Hence, it is only used when no more room is available for allocating more nodes. Otherwise, the program is simply let to run its course.

There are three main parts to the entire process known as garbage collection.

1) Mark cells that are in use;

2) Collect the unmarked cells and join them to the available space;

3) If necessary, compact the in-use space, i.e., translate those cells, and, finally, undo the marking.

14.2 MARKING PHASE

14.2.1 DETERMINING GARBAGE

In the garbage collection process, a basic presupposition is that it can be determined what is garbage and what is not.

— Memory locations are not garbage (i.e., they are active) if they are parts of nodes directly accessible (through a specific pointer variable) or indirectly accessible (by being accessible from another non-garbage node). Memory locations are also not garbage if they are scalar variables or arrays.

— All memory locations not accessible are considered "garbage."

14.2.2 MARKING ALGORITHM

Some way of marking a cell is needed, and usually this is achieved by using one bit (of a word) as a flag. Sometimes a pointer can be negated, especially if a program is simulating dynamic storage in an array.

The *marking algorithm* is summarized in the following three steps:

1) Mark all scalar and array variables;

2) Mark all pointer variables;

3) For evey pointer variable, traverse all nodes it leads to (using a version of depth-first search), and mark each of them.

Step 3 can cause problems and requires careful programming. Traversing a tree or a list is most easily done recursively. But recursive code, when executed, uses an internal stack that dynamically uses memory space. Unfortunately, the marking algorithm is done as part of garbage collection, and thus is performed only when there is very little space left in memory.

Thus, marking algorithms are written so that they run with very little additional space needed for variables, if any. As a result, the algorithm can be rather slow. A common algorithm includes double traversal of linked structures, including a temporary reversal of links.

14.3 COLLECTION AND COMPACTION

After the marking phase, the next step of garbage collection goes through memory and collects all unmarked (i.e., unused) cells, and then links them together to be able to be used again. This can be done by a simple sweep of memory, linking all unmarked cells to each other, while ignoring all marked cells.

Especially when a program has run awhile and has allocated and de-allocated numerous blocks of memory, the available sections of memory may be scattered throughout memory. Taken together, there may be a lot of memory available, but each individual section may be quite small. In this case, even a moderately sized array (if one needs to be allocated when a procedure is called) may not be able to be stored, since arrays need to be stored sequentially in one contiguous section of memory. This situation is called *memory fragmentation*. To remedy this, a process called *compaction* is sometimes used after the collection phase, which moves all "in use" memory locations to one contiguous section of memory, resulting in all the unused memory being together.

However, since pointers contain specific memory addresses, moving information in memory cells means having to re-address all pointers. Typically this is done by determining the new address of a node and then leaving a "forwarding" address in the old location. Then, the pointers are all updated by looking at the old location (still pointed to) and copying the new address left there. The exact order of each of these components may vary from algorithm to algorithm.

Typically, the compaction phase involves three passes:

1) Scan memory, computing and assigning new addresses to nodes in use;

2) Update all pointers;

3) Relocate all active nodes.

EXAMPLE
The following example depicts 10 blocks of memory. The various configurations can be described as follows:

A) Initial Configuration of Memory: it is unknown which blocks are not in use. It is known that block A is in use, though.

Name	Starting Location	Size	Links to:
A	100	50	E
B	150	275	H
C	425	25	G
D	450	282	F
E	732	18	C
F	750	61	–
G	811	39	I
H	850	100	D
I	950	50	–
J	1000	...	–

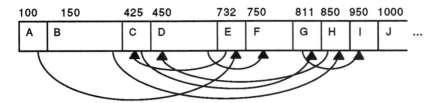

B) After the Marking Phase: it has been determined that the shaded blocks (B, D, F, H, and J) are not in use.

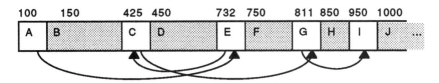

C) After Collection and Compaction: blocks A, C, E, G, and I have been moved to be contiguous. However, the final links from these blocks and other internal links all have to be re-addressed.

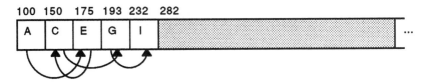

APPENDIX C

RECURSION VS. ITERATION

C–1 INTRODUCTION

In the vast majority of programs, some action or computation is usually repeated a number of times. There are two basic approaches to repetitive programming:

(1) iteration, and (2) recursion.

An **interative** program is one in which a loop (i.e., repetitive code) is explicit.

A **recursive** program is one in which there may not be any explicit loop, but in which a concept is defined (and computed) by calling itself.

Some concepts naturally are defined recursively, others can be expressed recursively, while still others cannot be (easily) expressed recursively. The basic mathematical operations can either be expressed recursively or by expansion in terms of a simpler operation (which can be considered as one form of iteration).

Factorial $n! = (1)(2)(3) \dots (n-1)(n)$
$= n(n-1)!$

(Here $n!$ is expressed in terms of a simpler version of itself, $(n-1)!$.)

Multiplication $ab = a(b-1) + a = \underbrace{a + a + a + a + \dots + a}_{b}$

(Here ab is expressed in terms of $a(b-1)$.)

Exponentiation $a^b = a^{(b-1)}a = \underbrace{a\,a\,a\,a \dots a}_{b}$

(Here a^b is expressed in terms of a^{b-1}.)

Every recursive definition must have some alternate definition for a fundamental case that does not involve itself. In the case of the three arithmetic operations just given, the following are the foundational values.

Factorial $1! = 0! = 1$
Multiplication $a1 = a$
Exponentiation $a^1 = a$

Many routines can be written in either an iterative version or a recursive version. Sometimes the iterative version is the one that has been developed as the fundamental algorithm and it is converted into a recursive version. Many times, however, the recursive version is the first one described, and then it is converted into an iterative form.

C–2 RECURSIVE BINARY SEARCH

In Section 5.3, an iterative version of binary search was presented in which in the loop new values of first and last were computed and the loop was re-executed with these new values. The following code is a recursive version of binary search. Notice that there is no loop, and that first and last are not re-calculated, but instead altered values (corresponding to first and last) are passed as parameters to the recursive call of the procedure.

```
PROCEDURE Binsearch(x:arraytype; first, last:INTEGER;
                            key:arrayitem; VAR place INTEGER);
VAR middle:INTEGER;
BEGIN
        IF first <= last THEN
            BEGIN
                middle := (first+last) DIV 2;
                IF key = x[middle] THEN
                    place := middle
                ELSE
                    IF key < x[middle] THEN
                        Binsearch(x, first, middle–1, key,place)
                    ELSE
                        Binsearch(x,middle+1,last,key,place)
                END (* IF first ... THEN *)
        ELSE
            place := 0
END;    (* Binsearch *)
```

Note: One begins by calling: Binsearch(x,1,n,key,place).

168

C-3 A NATURALLY RECURSIVE PROBLEM: FIBONACCI NUMBERS

The fibonacci sequence of numbers is defined recursively:

$$f_0 = f_1 = 1$$
$$f_n = f_{n-1} + f_{n-2} \text{ for } n \geq 2$$

This can easily be translated into a Pascal recursive function as follows:

```
FUNCTION fibon(n:INTEGER):INTEGER;
BEGIN
        IF n <= 1 THEN
            fibon := 1
        ELSE
            fibon := fibon(n–1) + fibon(n– 2)
END;
```

The following FORTRAN iterative version is a bit less intelligible.

```
    INTEGER FUNCTION FIBON(N)
    INTEGER F1,F2,TEMP,I,NM1,N
    F1=1
    F2=1
    NM1=N–1
    DO 10 I=1, NM1
        TEMP=F1+F2
        F1=F2
        F2=TEMP
10  CONTINUE
    FIBON=TEMP
    RETURN
    END
```

The relationship between the definition of fibonacci numbers and their computation is obscured in this iterative version. Whereas the recursive version follows the definition and calculates a number by starting at the desired number and going "back," the iterative version always starts at the beginning of the sequence (f_0 and f_1) and computes as much of the sequence as needed to get to the desired number. However, a method to "convert" recursive routines into iterative routines that retain some of the flavor of the recursive versions is given below in Section C-9.

C–4 OTHER SAMPLE ROUTINES

Here are two sets of subprograms in both recursive and iterative forms. Even though each form in either set does the same thing, the codes differ significantly and each iterative version shows little resemblance to the recursive one. They do show again, however, that recursive code lacks an explicit loop but has the recursive subprogram call, and that iterative code has an explicit loop.

GENERATING LISTS

RECURSIVE VERSION (same as code in Section 6.3.4)

```
FUNCTION Genlist(n:INTEGER):ptr;
VAR p:ptr;
BEGIN
      New(p);
      IF n > 1 THEN
          p^.next := Genlist(n–1)
      ELSE
          p^.next := NIL;
      p^.info := n;
      Genlist := p
END;   (* Genlist *)
```

170

ITERATIVE VERSION

```
FUNCTION Genlist(n:INTEGER):ptr;
VAR p,q:ptr;
        i : INTEGER;
BEGIN
        q := NIL;
        FOR i := 1 TO n DO
            BEGIN
                New(p);
                p^.info := i;
                p^.next := q;
                q := p
            END; (* FOR *)
        Genlist := q
END;    (* Genlist *)
```

PRINTING LISTS

RECURSIVE VERSION

```
PROCEDURE Printlist(list:ptr);
BEGIN
        IF list <> NIL THEN
            BEGIN
                Writeln(list^.info);
                Printlist(list^.next)
            END (* IF *)
END;    (* Printlist *)
```

INTERATIVE VERSION (same as code in Section 6.3.4)

```
PROCEDURE Printlist(list:ptr);
BEGIN
        WHILE list <> NIL DO
```

171

```
        BEGIN
                Writeln(list^.info);
                list := list^.next
        END (* While *)
END;    (* Printlist *)
```

C–5 "DIVIDE AND CONQUER" TECHNIQUES

"Divide and Conquer" techniques refer to those methods of solving problems that reduce a larger problem to simpler problems. These techniques are often associated with recursive programming since, by nature, recursive definitions are in some sense already "divide and conquer" definitions, defining a concept in terms of a (simpler) version of itself. Thus, to calculate $n!$, one can do the simpler problem of calculating $(n - 1)!$, followed by the simpler problem of multiplying n times $(n - 1)!$.

"Divide and Conquer" techniques can be summarized as follows:

— To do Problem A of size n,

   A) [Limit case] How is Problem A done with size just equal to 1?

   B) [Recursive case] How is Problem A done for "one more," given a way to do it for a smaller size? In other words, can "doing A" be converted into "doing A for size n assuming that it can be done for size $n - 1$"?

For example, to compute $n!$,

   A) The base case is computed: $1! = 1$.

B) It is recognized that to calculate $n!$, one can calculate $(n - 1)!$ and then multiply it by n.

C–6 THE TOWERS OF HANOI

The Towers of Hanoi is a puzzle-type game involving a board with three upright pegs, and a number of disks each with a center hole enabling them to be slipped onto any peg. The disks are of different sizes with no two disks being the same size. Initially, all the disks are on one peg arranged in order with the largest on the bottom and the smallest on the top.

The object of the game is to move all the disks to another peg, with the following rules (constraints):

1) Only one disk can be moved at a time.

2) A larger disk cannot be put on a smaller one.

The problem is solved by applying a "divide and conquer" technique and coming up with a recursive solution.

SOLUTION FOR 1 DISK: Move one disk (the bottom and only one) from one peg to the destination peg.

SOLUTION FOR 2 DISKS:

1) Move the smaller disk to an auxiliary peg,

2) move the larger (bottom) disk to the destination peg,

3) then move the smaller disk to the destination peg (on top of the larger disk).

GENERAL SOLUTION: The general solution can be seen after analyzing a few more particular solutions. However, the emerging pattern can be seen here:

Moving 5 disks from A to C (with auxiliary peg B) *is basically the same as*

1) moving 4 disks from A to B (with auxiliary peg C),

2) moving the largest (bottom) disk from A to C,

3) then moving 4 disks from B to C (with auxiliary peg A).

This can be coded as follows in Pascal:

```
PROCEDURE Hanoi(n:posint;frompeg,topeg,auxpeg:char);
BEGIN
        IF n=1 THEN
                Writeln('move disk 1 from peg', frompeg,
                      '  to peg',topeg)
        ELSE
                BEGIN
                      Hanoi(n-1,frompeg,auxpeg,topeg);
                      Writeln('move disk',n,'   from peg',frompeg,
                            '  to peg',topeg);
                      Hanoi(n-1,auxpeg,topeg,frompeg);
                END
END;
```

The main program would merely be:

```
BEGIN
        Hanoi(5,'a','c','b')
END.
```

Although the "divide and conquer technique" may seem complicated as far as trying to understand the logic is concerned, it is much simpler than initially trying to develop an iterative version.

C–7 EVALUATING RECURSIVE FUNCTIONS

There are two ways of evaluating recursive functions. When given a mathematical definition, it is often better to evaluate it iteratively, starting at the beginning. When given a segment of recursive code, it may have to be evaluated recursively, with care taken that none of the returns are skipped. The following are offered as examples.

EXAMPLE #1

Let a new (recursive) function be defined as follows:

$$t(n) = \begin{cases} 1 & \text{if } n = 0,1,2 \\ t(n-1)+t(n-2)+t(n-3) & \text{for } n \geq 3 \end{cases}$$

Then, starting with the first (foundational) values, the subsequent values for the function can be computed iteratively:

$t(0) = 1$	$t(3) = 3$	$t(6) = 17$
$t(1) = 1$	$t(4) = 5$	$t(7) = 31$
$t(2) = 1$	$t(5) = 9$	$t(8) = 57$

EXAMPLE #2

Given the following subprogram, evaluation must take place recursively:

```
PROCEDURE Mystery;
VAR value:CHAR;
```

```
BEGIN
        Read(value);
        IF NOT Eoln THEN Mystery;
        Write(value)
END;
```

INPUT: Cat

It is often best to imagine that the code is repeated however many times are needed to accomplish the task. To demonstrate, the code will be abbreviated by the first key word of each line. The number after each keyword indicates the order in which the statement is executed.

READ (1) (value:=C)	READ (3) (value:=a)	READ (5) (value:=t)
IF (2)	IF (4)	IF (6)
WRITE (9)	WRITE (8)	WRITE (7)

Thus the output is: taC,. since the three Write statements are done in reverse order compared to the Reads.

Oftentimes, trees are helpful in analyzing the program flow of a recursive routine. Each node indicates a call to the recursive routine, and a node has as many children as there are recursive calls to itself. Trees can thus provide a handy way to analyze the total number of calls to a recursive routine and thus the total amount of work done by a routine. For example, if a recursive procedure always calls itself twice (unless the base option is chosen), then it can be depicted as a binary tree and the total number of nodes in the tree is the same as the number of times the procedure is called.

C–8 RECURSION AND STACKS

When a subprogram is called, a number of actions are performed internally by a computer:

1. Arguments are passed;

2. Local variables are (allocated and) initialized;

3. Control is transferred to the subprogram code.

Step 3, transferring control, consists both of jumping to the memory address of the subprogram code, and also remembering (i.e., storing) the return address (i.e., where the program continues after the subprogram finishes).

In languages like Pascal in which recursion is possible, instead of single memory locations being created when a subprogram is called, stacks are used for subprogram variables and for the return address. Only one copy of the subprogram code exists and the "repeated" variables and return addresses are stored on stacks. Thus, even though the procedure followed in the second example of the previous section helps to visualize the program flow, it may confuse what is actually happening.

Suppose the code corresponded to these indicated memory locations:

Memory location
2581	Read(value);
2582	IF NOT Eoln THEN Mystery;
2585	Write(value)

It can be envisioned that two stacks would be used, one to store the return address and one to store all the values of the variable *value*. After *Read(value)* had read the last letter of the input *Cat*, the stacks would look like:

Stacks

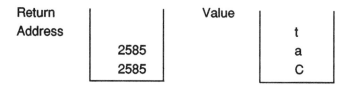

Return Address | | | 2585 | 2585 |

Value | | t | a | C |

Write(value) would output only the top of the stack, and hence the output would be the reverse of the input. When an instance of the recursive subprogram is done, the return address stack is popped and control is transferred to the address popped off the stack. The variable stacks are also popped but their values are simply discarded.

C–9 CONVERTING RECURSIVE CODE TO ITERATIVE

Recursive code can always be converted to iterative code by explicitly including in the code a stack to store all necessary variable values. Sometimes the conversion is difficult, especially if the code is complex. This section attempts to show a conversion method that works in many cases.

Given a recursive procedure in the form:

```
        PROCEDURE  Recur (n,a,b);
        BEGIN
(a–1)          IF BaseCondition THEN
(a–2)              Write('something')
               ELSE
                  BEGIN
(1)                  Recur (n–1,a–1,b);
```

178

```
(2)                       Recur(n–1,a,b–1)
                  END
        END
```

This can be converted to an iterative version in this form:

```
         PROCEDURE  Iter (n,b,c);
         BEGIN
(c–1)           InitializeStack(S);
(c–2)           Push3(n,b,c,S);
(c–3)           WHILE NOT EndCondition DO
                  BEGIN
(c–4)               Pop3(n,b,c,S);
(a–1)               IF BaseCondition THEN
(a-2)                  Write('something')
                    ELSE
                      BEGIN
(2*)                     Push3(n–1,a,b–1,S);
(1*)                     Push3(n–1,a–1,b,S)
                      END
                  END    (* WHILE *)
         END;
```

Notice the following: (a) The order of the recursive statements (1) and (2) have been interchanged in the iterative version and changed into statements that push the arguments onto the stack; (b) the stack is modified to enable the storing of three values (hence the operations Push3 and Pop3).

Sometimes a more complicated program can be converted first. The following is an alternave version of the towers of Hanoi program in which statement (a–2) has been simplified and statement (2) (formerly a Write) has been replaced by another call to HanoiB with n having the value of 1 (which does only a Write).

```
        PROCEDURE  HanoiB(n:posint;frompeg,
                         topeg,auxpeg:char);
        BEGIN
(a–1)        If n=1 THEN
(a-2)            Writeln('move top disk from peg',frompeg,
                     '  to peg   ',topeg)
             ELSE
             BEGIN
(1)              HanoiB(n–1,frompeg,auxpeg,topeg);
(2)              HanoiB(  1,frompeg,topeg,auxpeg);
(3)              HanoiB(n–1,auxpeg,topeg,frompeg);
             END
        END;
```

This can be converted to the following iterative program using the scheme given above.

```
        PROCEDURE  Hanoilt(n:posint;frompeg,topeg,
                         auxpeg:char);
        BEGIN
(c–1)        InitializeStack(S);
(c–2)        Push4(n,frompeg,topeg,auxpeg,S);
(c–3)        WHILE NOT Empty(S) DO
             BEGIN
(c–4)            Pop4(n,frompeg,topeg,auxpeg,S);
(a–1)            If n=1 THEN
(a–2)                Writeln('move top disk from peg',
                         frompeg,'  to peg   ', topeg)
                 ELSE
                 BEGIN
(3*)                 Push4(n–1,auxpeg,topeg,frompeg);
(2*)                 Push4(  1, frompeg,topeg,auxpeg);
(1*)                 Push4(n–1,frompeg,auxpeg,topeg)
                 END
             END
        END;
```

If such a transformation of the original code is not possible, and a non-recursive statement comes between two recursive calls, sometimes the iterative version can be made to include a flag indicating the type of statement that should be executed. In the following code to print the inorder traversal of a tree, the recursive section has two types of statements: (1) the recursive call, and (2) the write statement. Since there is no explicit base condition, there is no way to re-code the Write statement. In the iterative version, the parameter for the Write statement is stored on the stack with the label 0, whereas the parameter for the recursive call is stored with the label 1. This label is tested before the stack section is entered.

Recursive version:

```
       PROCEDURE  Inprint(t:tree);
       BEGIN
(a)            IF t <> NIL THEN
                   BEGIN
(1)                    Inprint(t^.left);
(2)                    Write(t^.info);
(3)                    Inprint(t^.right)
                   END
       END;
```

Iterative version:

```
       PROCEDURE Inprintlt(t:tree);
       VAR s:stack;
       BEGIN
(c-1)          InitializeStack (S);
(c-2)          Push2(t,1,S);
(c-3)          WHILE NOT Empty(S) DO
                   BEGIN
(c-4)                  Pop2(t,id,S);
```

181

```
(a)                        IF t <> nil THEN
                              IF id = 0 THEN Write (t^.info)
                              ELSE
                              BEGIN
(3*)                                 Push2(t^.right,1,S);
(2*)                                 Push2(t,0,S);
(1*)                                 Push2(t^.left,1,S)
                              END
                      END
          END;
```

Arithmetic statements may take a bit of creativity in conversion. The recursive call in the following code for computing factorials is to a FUNCTION that is part of an assignment statement. In the iterative version, that assignment statement becomes a WHILE loop.

```
          FUNCTION Fact(i:INTEGER):INTEGER;
          BEGIN
                IF i = 0 THEN
                    Fact := 1
                ELSE
                    Fact := i*Fact(i-1)
          END;
```

This can be slightly re-written by adding a temporary variable:

```
          FUNCTION Fact(i:INTEGER):INTEGER;
          VAR temp:INTEGER;
          BEGIN
(a-1)         IF i = 0 THEN
(a-2)             temp := 1
              ELSE
(1)               temp := i*Fact(i-1);
(b)           Fact := temp;
          END;
```

Iterative version:

```
        FUNCTION FactIt(i:INTEGER):INTEGER;
        VAR temp:INTEGER;
              s : stack;
        BEGIN
(c–1)         InitializeStack(S);
              temp := 0;
                 (* needed for the arithmetic calculation *)
(c–2)         Push(i,S);
(c–3)         WHILE NOT Empty(S) DO
                 BEGIN
(c–4)              i := Pop(S);
(a–1)              IF i = 0 then
(a–2)                 temp := 1
                   ELSE
                   BEGIN
                     IF I <> 0 THEN Push(i,S);
                        (* check last value Pushed
                           and re-Push *)
                     IF temp = 0 THEN
                        Push(i–1,S)
                        (* temp=0 as long as i >= 1 —
                           store parameters to Fact *)
                     ELSE
                        WHILE NOT Empty(S) DO
(1*)                       temp := temp*Pop(S)
                   END;
                 END;
(b)           Fact:=temp
        END;
```

183

APPENDIX D

ALGEBRAIC NOTATION

D–1 ALGEBRAIC ORDERS AND TREE TRAVERSALS

When writing an algebraic expression consisting of a binary operator applied to its two operands (i.e., arguments), three standard orders of operators and operands are used. The names of these three orders are related to the placement of the operator relative to the two operands.

		Example:
PREFIX	**operator** first-operand second-operand	+ a b
POSTFIX	first-operand second operand **operator**	a b +
INFIX	first-operand **operator** second-operand	a + b

These three orders are also related to tree traversal orders seen in Section 10.2. The second tree shown in Section 10.2 has operators as the information stored in the interior nodes. The tree traversals listed there correspond to the three orders listed in this section. Thus, the preorder traversal of that tree gives an algebraic expression in prefix order, and so on.

COMMENTS

1) PREFIX order is "functional notation" — the mathematical order used when writing functions of two variables, e.g., $f(a,b) = a + b$ could also be written $+(a, b)$. This is also the standard order used in the programming language LISP, widely used for artificial intelligence work.

2) INFIX order is the standard arithmetic notation order, e.g., $a + b$.

3) POSTFIX order is also called RPN order, e.g., $a, b, +$. RPN is the abbreviation for *R*everse *P*olish *N*otation, developed by the Polish mathematician Jan Lukasiewicz. It is also the order used by certain types of calculators. In these machines, a stack is used to store the operands (i.e., numbers) and these are combined when an operator is indicated. These types of calculators are recognized by the absence of an equals key.

D–2 GENERAL CONVERSION RULES

Conversion between the various algebraic orders is usually accomplished by first fully parenthesizing the expression. In other words, parentheses are inserted so that there is one set of each operator. For example,

#1	normal algebraic:	A+B*C
	fully parenthesized:	(A+(B*C))

#2	normal algebraic:	(A+B)*C
	fully parenthesized:	((A+B)*C)

To convert from infix to postfix (prefix),

1) fully parenthesize the expression,

2) move operator to the right (left) parenthesis that corresponds to it,

3) and then remove all parentheses.

Continuing the previous examples:

#1   fully parenthesized: (A+(B*C))
        RPN   (A(B C*)+) = ABC*+

#2   fully parenthesized: ((A+B)*C)
        RPN   ((A B+) C*) = AB+C*

Conversion from postfix (prefix) to infix is done in a similar way, but "fully parenthesizing" a postfix or prefix expression is significantly more complicated.

Starting with a postfix (prefix) expression, a set of parentheses is included around the outside and a right (left) parenthesis after (before) each operator. Then the expression is scanned from the center toward the other side, inserting a matching parenthesis every time two operands have been identified corresponding to each operator. The process is illustrated in the following example which fully parenthesizes A B C + D * +.

     (A B C + D * +)   Outer parentheses inserted.
     (A B C +)D *) +)   Right parenthesis next to each operator.
     (A B C +)D *) +)   First pair of operands identified.
       ^1 2 o^
     (A(B C +)D) +)   First left parenthesis inserted.
     (A (B C +)D *)+)   Next pair of operands identified.
       ^   1   2 0^   (Note the first operand is an entire
                        expression: (B C +).)
     (A((B C +)D *)+)   Second left parenthesis inserted.

The expression is now fully parenthesized.

To convert from postfix (prefix) to infix,

1) fully parenthesize the expression,

2) move the operator of each group in between its operands,

3) and then remove unnecessary parentheses.

Continuing the example above,

fully parenthesized:	(A((B C +)D *)+)
with moved operators:	(A+((B+C)* D))
unnecessary parentheses removed:	A + (B+C)*D

NOTES

1) With infix expressions, all parentheses may not always be able to be removed.

2) When converting from one order to another order, the order of the operands (arguments) always stays the same.

3) The changes in the expression include the order of the operators, the presence or absence of parentheses, and the position of the operators relative to their own operands.

D–3 CONVERSION ALGORITHMS AND INFIX PRECEDENCE RULES

Converting the procedures just outlined into an algorithm that can be programmed involves recognizing, in particular, that (1) the process of "fully parenthesizing" an expression is only needed to identify which operator belongs to which operands (arguments); (2) the order of the operands remains the same in each of the orders (only the order of the operators changes); and (3) in infix notation, auxiliary "rules" are needed to help determine the order in which the operators are evaluated.

These auxiliary rules, usually called *precedence rules*, are needed in infix expressions since, otherwise, expressions like $A + B*C$ may be erroneously evaluated (since the second operator is evaluated before the first). However, such rules are not needed in postfix or prefix expressions. For example, $A\ B\ C\ *\ +$ is unambiguous — the operators are always evaluated left to right, as printed. Similarly, $+\ A\ *\ B\ C$ is also unambiguous — the operators are always evaluated in reverse order, from right to left. (Note that all three expressions denote the same reality.)

According to these precedence rules, multiplication and division are said to "take precedence over" or "have a higher precedence than" addition and subtraction, and exponentiation takes precedence over multiplication. Thus, given $A + B*C^D$, C^D is evaluated first, then the result multiplied by B, and finally the addition is performed last. The use of parentheses can alter the order of precedence since what is interior to a set of parentheses takes precedence over the exterior operator. Thus, given $(A + B)^C$, the addition is performed first because the parenthetical expression has higher precedence than even exponentiation.

Many algorithms for converting infix to postfix evaluate precedence in some way. If an operator has lower precedence than its successor, it is stored on a stack until the successor is evaluted first. A lower precedence operator is never put on top of a higher precedence operator in the stack. The stack is first reduced, by operators being popped off. Algorithms handle parentheses in various ways. The following general plan of an algorithm always stores left parentheses on the stack and incorporates both parentheses into the precedence rules. The right parenthesis has lower precedence than any operator. This results in the right parenthesis never being stored and it forces the stack to be reduced (i.e., popped) until a corresponding left parenthesis appears.

GENERAL PLAN OF ALGORITHM

STAGE I — Read in the input line, character by character.
```
WHILE (there are more input characters) DO
    Read(NewCharacter)
    IF (NewCharacter is an operand) THEN
    |   Write(NewCharacter to the output string)
    ELSE (* NewCharacter is an operator or parenthesis *)
        Continue := TRUE
        WHILE (stack is not empty AND top of stack has
               precedence over NewCharacter AND Continue) DO
            OldOperator := Pop(stack)
            Continue := FALSE
            If (OldOperator is not a left parenthesis) THEN
            |   Continue := TRUE
            |__ |__ Write(OldOperator to the output string)
        IF (NewCharacter is not a right parenthesis) THEN
    |__ |__ |  Push(NewCharacter, stack)
```

STAGE II — Empty the stack (when there is no more input.)
```
WHILE (stack is not empty) DO
    OldOperator := Pop(stack)
    IF (OldOperator is not a left parenthesis) THEN
    |__ |__ Write(OldOperator to the output string)
```

This algorithm thus remembers the "more important" (i.e., higher precedence) operators by storing them on the stack, and then outputs them when needed (sometimes even in reverse order).

D–4 ALGORITHM EXAMPLES

EXAMPLE 1: INPUT STRING: A + B * C

step	input symbol	complete output	Stack (right-most is top-of-stack)
1	A	A	
2	+	A	+
3	B	A B	+
4	*	A B	+ *
5	C	A B C	+ * ___(no more input)
6		A B C *	+
7		A B C * +	

$$A + B * C \Rightarrow A B C * +$$

Note the reversed order.

EXAMPLE 2: INPUT STRING: (A + B) * C

step	input symbol	complete output	Stack (right-most is top-of-stack)
1	(		(
2	A	A	(
3	+	A	(+
4	B	A B	(+
5	)	A B +	
6	*	A B +	*
7	C	A B + C	* ____(no more input)
8		A B + C *	

APPENDIX E

LARGE INTEGER ARITHMETIC

E-1 COMPUTER LIMITATIONS

Sometimes extended precision accuracy is needed, for example, when trying to calculate e or π to 200 decimal places. Such numbers require special formulae to generate the numbers, and they must be stored in segments with special data structures. This approach is necessary since even using languages that have double (or even extended) precision real arithmetic (like FORTRAN), most computers rarely give more than 30 digits accuracy. Some machines cannot store integers larger than a few billion (10 digits). Hence the computation of π to 200 decimal places or even the computation of 13! (over six billion) is impossible without special programming techniques.

When using extended precision accuracy, it is usually easier to work with integers. This can be done even when dealing with real numbers if the decimal point is simply ignored for purposes of calculation and then inserted when needed after the computation is completed. An appropriate choice of data structures can help to simplify both data storage and numeric computation.

When dealing with extended prevision numbers by means of large integers, the approach taken most often is to subdivide the large integer into smaller pieces, each of which can be stored in the computer without any problem. Then the normal arithmetic operations are performed, section by section, observing the standard rules for "overflow" and "carry." The problem is that the arithmetic operations must be coded by the programmer rather than left to the hardware of the computer.

The normal data structure chosen to implement large integers is a linked list or an array.

A problem like this shows both the limitations of computers for many problems, as well as the necessity of carefully using data structures in programs. This problem requires a programmer to understand simple arithmetic operations (like multiplication and addition) that are normally taken for granted. It also necessitates a careful choice of data structures and a careful manipulation of the information stored.

E–2 ADDING LARGE INTEGERS

The following problem can be done (by hand) simply, in the usual digit-by-digit manner.

```
      1 0 9   8 5 1   8 6 2
  +             3 6   9 7 5
      ─────────────────────
      1 0 9   8 8 8   8 3 7
```

These two integers (addends) can also be broken up so that each segment is less than 100 (i.e., each segment is 2 digits long). These segments can then be stored in two different linked lists, such that the smallest value (column) digits come first (i.e., the head node contains the digits in the 1's and 10's

192

columns, the next node contains the digits in the 100's and 1000's columns, etc.).

Therefore: 109851862 ⇔ list p ⇔

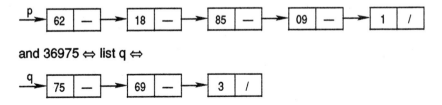

and 36975 ⇔ list q ⇔

To add the large integers, the entries in the two lists are added, node by node, starting with the head nodes. After each new sum is computed, a check is made to see that the sum remains less than 100 and a carry of 1 is added to the next set of nodes, if necessary. The computed sum (mod 100) is stored in a new sum list, *s*. If one list runs out of nodes before the other one does, the remaining values in the other list are transferred to the sum list (always keeping watch of the carry).

p →	62 →	18 →	85 →	09 →	1
q →	75 →	69 →	3	—	—
carry	0	1	0	0	0
	—	—	—	—	—
Sum	137	88	88	09	1
s →	37 →	88 →	88 →	09 →	1

This can be implemented by a linked list, a circular linked list, or even a doubly-linked list. If a specific problem is dealing with a maximum number of digits, say 300, then it is sometimes easier to use an array as the underlying data structure.

E–3 MULTIPLYING LARGE INTEGERS

An example of multiplying two integers is presented first to allow some analysis of what happens.

```
          1 2 3 4 1 2
×           2 3 1 4 2
        ─────────────
          2 4 6 8 2 4
        4 9 3 6 4 8 –      (adding gives)   5 1 8 3 3 0 4
      1 2 3 4 1 2 – –
      3 7 0 2 3 6 – – –    (adding gives)   3 8 2 5 7 7 2
    2 4 6 8 2 4 – – – –           →           2 4 6 8 2 4
    ─────────────────────
    2 8 5 6 0 0 0 5 0 4
```

It is also possible to break the factors into two-digit groups and multiply the numbers, group-by-group (rather than digit-by-digit). This process will also produce a correct answer, just as in the case of addition.

	12	34	12	
×	2	31	42	
	504	1428	504	
372	1054	372	–	Convert these numbers to num-
24	68	24	–	– bers < 100 and add the "carries"
5	18	33	04	to the next section to the left.
3	82	57	72	–
24	68	24	–	–
28	56	00	05	04

Notice that these numbers are identical to the summed groups on the right above.

Notice the answer is the same as that above. (For future reference, the first two intermediate sums add up to 3 87 76 05 04.)

This example is an attempt to motivate the following. If the two factors are subdivided into two digit segments, and the segments are stored in lists as was done previously in the discussion on addition, multiplication can be performed group-by-group, and the answer stored in a produce list s.

However, unlike the addition process, in multiplication, repeated multiplications and additions to s must be performed. In other words, the first node (i.e., the last segment) of q must be multiplied by the entire p list. Then, the second node of q is multiplied by the p list, and so on. This corresponds to multiplying the first number digit-by-digit by the second number. This process is now depicted with the numbers given above.

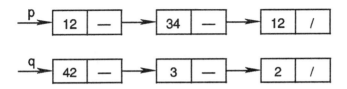

Pass 1: (all of p) times (segment 1 of q = 42)

	12×42	34×42	12×42	
	504	1428	504	
carry	0	5	15	5
	504	1433	518	5
s→	04 →	33 →	18 →	5

NOTE: This is the same as the first partial sum above.

Now shift the starting node of s to #2.

Pass 2: (all of p) times (segment 2 of q = 31)

	12×31	34×31	12×31	
	372	1054	372	
carry	0	4	10	3

OLD s 04 →
$$\frac{33}{405} \to \frac{18}{1076} \to \frac{5}{387} \quad \underline{\quad} \atop 3$$

NEW s 04 → 05 → 76 → 87 → 3

NOTE: This is the same as the second partial sum above.

Now shift the starting node of s to #3.

Pass 3: (all of p) times (segment 3 of q = 2)

	12×2	34×2	12×2
	24	68	24
carry	0	1	1
OLD s 04 → 05 →	76 →	87 →	3
	100	156	28

NEW s 04 → 05 → 00 → 56 → 28

There are no more segments to shift over to in q. The process is completed.

The answer is (reading s "backwards") 2856000504 (same as both times above).

E–4 DIVIDING INTEGERS TO AN ARBITRARY PRECISION

Once again, it is good to examine the old grammar school methods of arithmetic before writing computer code. First, an example of a normal "long" division (dividing one by seven) is given.

```
                   .  1   4   2   8   5   7   1   ...
      7)   1   .   0
                   7
                   3   0
                   2   8
                       2   0
                       1   4
                           6   0
                           5   6
                               4   0
                               3   5
                                   5   0
                                   4   9
                                       1   0
                                       7
                                       ...
```

PASCAL CODE

```
Write ('0.');
modulus := 10;
divisor := 7;
number := 10;
FOR i := i TO limit DO
    BEGIN
        remainder := number MOD divisor;
        quotient := number DIV divisor;
        Write(quotient:1);
        number := remainder*modulus
    END;
Writeln;
```

The example above works with the modulus being equal to
the base of the number. However, a larger modulus may also
be used as in the case of addition and multiplication.

$$
\begin{array}{r}
.\quad 14\quad 28\quad 57\quad 14\quad \ldots \\ \hline
7)\ 1\ .\ \ 00 \\
98 \\ \hline
2\quad 00 \\
1\quad 96 \\ \hline
4\quad 00 \\
3\quad 99 \\ \hline
1\quad 00 \\
98 \\ \hline
2\quad \ldots
\end{array}
$$

This shows that modular arithmetic also works for division as well.

Note: In some situations, to divide large integers, e.g., a/b, it may be easier to first find $1/b$ and then to multiply a by $(1/b)$.

INDEX

HANDBOOK AND GUIDE FOR
COMPARING and SELECTING
COMPUTER LANGUAGES

BASIC	PL/1
FORTRAN	APL
PASCAL	ALGOL-60
COBOL	C

- This book is the first of its kind ever produced in computer science.

- It examines and highlights the differences and similarities among the eight most widely used computer languages.

- A practical guide for selecting the most appropriate programming language for any given task.

- Sample programs in all eight languages are written and compared side-by-side. Their merits are analyzed and evaluated.

- Comprehensive glossary of computer terms.

Available at your local bookstore or order directly from us by sending in coupon below.

RESEARCH and EDUCATION ASSOCIATION
61 Ethel Road W., Piscataway, New Jersey 08854
Phone: (201) 819-8880

VISA   MasterCard

Charge Card Number

Please check one box:
- ☐ Payment enclosed
- ☐ Visa
- ☐ Master Card

Expiration Date _____ / _____
               Mo   Yr

Please ship the "Computer Languages Handbook" @ $8.95 plus $2.00 for shipping.

Name _____

Address _____

City _____ State _____ Zip _____

THE PROBLEM SOLVERS

The "PROBLEM SOLVERS" are comprehensive supplemental textbooks designed to save time in finding solutions to problems. Each "PROBLEM SOLVER" is the first of its kind ever produced in its field. It is the product of a massive effort to illustrate almost any imaginable problem in exceptional depth, detail, and clarity. Each problem is worked out in detail with step-by-step solution, and the problems are arranged in order of complexity from elementary to advanced. Each book is fully indexed for locating problems rapidly.

ADVANCED CALCULUS
ALGEBRA & TRIGONOMETRY
AUTOMATIC CONTROL
  SYSTEMS/ROBOTICS
BIOLOGY
BUSINESS, MANAGEMENT,
  & FINANCE
CALCULUS
CHEMISTRY
COMPLEX VARIABLES
COMPUTER SCIENCE
DIFFERENTIAL EQUATIONS
ECONOMICS
ELECTRICAL MACHINES
ELECTRIC CIRCUITS
ELECTROMAGNETICS
ELECTRONIC COMMUNICATIONS
ELECTRONICS
FINITE & DISCRETE MATH
FLUID MECHANICS/DYNAMICS
GENETICS

GEOMETRY:
PLANE · SOLID · ANALYTIC
HEAT TRANSFER
LINEAR ALGEBRA
MACHINE DESIGN
MECHANICS : STATICS · DYNAMICS
NUMERICAL ANALYSIS
OPERATIONS RESEARCH
OPTICS
ORGANIC CHEMISTRY
PHYSICAL CHEMISTRY
PHYSICS
PRE-CALCULUS
PSYCHOLOGY
STATISTICS
STRENGTH OF MATERIALS &
  MECHANICS OF SOLIDS
TECHNICAL DESIGN GRAPHICS
THERMODYNAMICS
TRANSPORT PHENOMENA :
MOMENTUM · ENERGY · MASS
VECTOR ANALYSIS

If you would like more information about any of these books, complete the coupon below and return it to us or go to your local bookstore.

The Essentials of
ACCOUNTING & BUSINESS®

Each book in the **Accounting and Business ESSENTIALS** series offers all essential information about the subject it covers. It includes every important principle and concept, and is designed to help students in preparing for exams and doing homework. The **Accounting and Business ESSENTIALS** are excellent supplements to any class text or course of study.

The **Accounting and Business ESSENTIALS** are complete and concise, with quick access to needed information. They also provide a handy reference source at all times. The **Accounting and Business ESSENTIALS** are prepared with REA's customary concern for high professional quality and student needs.

Available titles include:
Accounting I & II
Advanced Accounting
Business Law I & II
Cost & Managerial Accounting I & II
Financial Management
Intermediate Accounting I & II
Microeconomics
Macroeconomics I & II
Marketing Principles
Money & Banking I & II

If you would like more information about any of these books, complete the coupon below and return it to us or go to your local bookstore.